MW00700590

'Weintraub and Lewis' *InCredible Communication* provides a blueprint by which each of us can learn to refine and leverage our communication skills at a time when they are needed more than ever.'

Willow Bay, Dean,
USC Annenberg School for Communication and Journalism

'*InCredible Communication* is the book I've been waiting for. This take-action book is filled with hands-on, practical communication tools to manage your reputation, your context and the story you want to tell about yourself.'

Ron Ricci, Founder and CEO,
The Transparency Imperative

'Weintraub and Lewis have laid out a clear plan for action for navigating today's very complicated world which requires even more finely honed communication skills than ever before. It's a book that I will refer to over and over again.'

Carol Nygren, SVP
Strategic Business Development, Cityneon Holdings

'Whether you are just starting your career or are at the top of your game leading an organization, *InCredible Communication* will provide you with the insights and actionable tools necessary to be a credible and effective communicator and leader.'

Vince Klaseus, President,
Universal Brand Development, NBCUniversal

InCredible
COMMUNICATION

Uncover the Invaluable Art of Selling Yourself

**Steven Lewis &
Rebecca Weintraub, PhD.**

BLOOMSBURY BUSINESS
LONDON • OXFORD • NEW YORK • NEW DELHI • SYDNEY

BLOOMSBURY BUSINESS
Bloomsbury Publishing Plc
50 Bedford Square, London, WC1B 3DP, UK
29 Earlsfort Terrace, Dublin 2, Ireland

BLOOMSBURY, BLOOMSBURY BUSINESS and the Diana logo are trademarks
of Bloomsbury Publishing Plc

First published in Great Britain 2022

A catalogue record for this book is available from the British Library

Library of Congress Cataloging-in-Publication data has been applied for

ISBN: HB: 978-1-4729-9172-0; eBook: 978-1-4729-9171-3

2 4 6 8 10 9 7 5 3 1

Typeset by Deanta Global Publishing Services, Chennai, India
Printed and bound in Great Britain by CPI Group (UK) Ltd, Croydon CR0 4YY

To find out more about our authors and books visit www.bloomsbury.com
and sign up for our newsletters

We dedicate this book to our parents.

To the memories of my mothers, Goody Kallner Weintraub and Blossom Golin Weintraub who, as teachers, understood the importance of communication, and fostered my writing and speaking talents and by doing so, made this book possible.

Rebecca Weintraub

To my father Joe, who as an inventor, entrepreneur, and marketer always told me that the key to success was always the relationships you make, and the most meaningful relationships are always built on a foundation of honesty and clear messaging.

Steven Lewis

Contents

Foreword
by Kevin Lynch, Optiv CEO

We remember great leaders by the words they use. More, we remember how those words made us feel. The power of storytelling, and the credibility and authenticity of how that story is delivered, can inspire, unite and serve as a catalyst for positive change.

The fundamental power of communication – so adeptly and famously employed by great leaders and storytellers like Winston Churchill, John F. Kennedy, Dr Martin Luther King Jr and so many more – is available to all of us. Personally, it has been the single most valuable instrument in my 'executive toolbox', because it is the *only* way for me to effectively engage, rally and unite a company of thousands around a shared mission.

I faced a leadership challenge on day one when I became CEO of Optiv Security. The former CEO had been in place for nearly two decades as a respected founding member of the company. I was coming in from one of the company's primary competitors and, to add icing to the cake, it was April 2020 – which to many marked the early and deep impact associated with the COVID-19 pandemic and work-from-home economy. So, there I was, a new guy from a rival firm who couldn't even meet with his team in person. Not an ideal situation.

I turned to the most powerful tool at my disposal – my voice.

In order to effectively communicate and reach my new employees, I knew I had to first embrace and connect with the corporate culture. Too many leaders come into new situations wanting to 'rip and replace' the corporate culture with something they like better. The problem with this approach is, you can't force culture to change – you can only *lead* it to change.

As this book states, understanding an organization's communication culture is key to being a credible and effective communicator within it. So I began to immerse myself in the corporate culture by listening to what people said, what motivated them, what frustrated them, what made them tick. I paid attention to how they spoke and how messages were written, delivered and received.

When you listen, one of the most under-utilized communication tools, you convey to people that their experience and opinions are important. You build trust by communicating that you're not someone who believes he has all the answers, and instead your method becomes transparent, gaining a greater understanding of a topic before making any substantive decisions.

My advice for readers, born at the intersection of personal experience and the rich lessons outlined within, is don't just rely on the executive team for input. Consistently seek input from people throughout the organization. Listening and storytelling are exceptional moments to break from traditional organizational hierarchy. Invite employees from all levels and functions into executive meetings and tell them you want to hear their opinions (and make it clear there will be no repercussions for critical opinion and stand by your words). Attend various organizational functions like department meetings, virtual conference calls and even group lunches. Stop people in the hallways to talk to them or send a message.

No matter your seniority, judiciously allocate part of your schedule to listen and engage with anyone in your organization. Proactively and consistently seek out diverse perspectives and communicate with them in a way where they feel heard, respected and valued – be their champion. When you've done that, you'll have laid the foundation of trust and they'll accept your leadership. Importantly, you can begin to rally everyone around a set of unifying values that motivates and empowers each and every person to lead.

I believe leadership isn't just about title or hierarchy. It's about how you inspire, how you teach, how you problem solve, how you lift up those around you and how you communicate through your values, actions and words.

When you take the time to understand a company's culture, you can use the right words and the right stories and anecdotes that resonate and tug on heartstrings, and that's when the magic happens.

Effective communication is the currency of effective leadership – whether you're an individual contributor, in charge of a small team, a department, or a multi-thousand-person company. And, anyone can learn to be a more effective communicator.

If communication is culture and culture is communication, *InCredible Communication* systematizes the path to becoming a better corporate culture communicator and leader. And really, the lessons learned can be applied to all aspects of our lives. We all have the power to become more effective leaders and make a positive difference in the lives of co-workers, friends, family members and our communities… simply by understanding the fundamentals of good communications and practically putting them to work.

Preface

We never know what will send us off on a journey.

Ours began in 2018 when Steven was invited to be interviewed for a podcast called *Produce Yourself,* hosted by Terence Michael. At the time, America was going through what could best be described as a credibility crisis. The questioning of what was accepted as fact was being blurred by rhetoric with terms like 'alternative facts' and 'fake news' and a general gaslighting of the nation. For Steven, a press representative, documentarian and corporate communication consultant who had always believed that one's personal credibility is their most valuable asset, the assault was mind-numbing. Throughout his career Steven repeatedly told his clients, who included Academy Award winning actors and Fortune 500 executives, an interview was the best opportunity to find out what you think and help you to reveal your passions. In this case Steven was the subject of the interview and the truth of that advice became even clearer to him. Steven realized what mattered to him was communication credibility – it was why he was being interviewed and it was what he wanted people to be thinking about.

Such was the beginning.

With a mission to wake those who had become lulled into questioning the importance of credibility, *InCredible Communication* was born. We both liked the double meaning of the title. Good communication has to be credible and incredible. Like so many journeys, this too had many bumps and diversions, but none more significant or beneficial to the project than the desire to elevate the theme from a pop culture, in-the-moment morality jolt to a more researched-based academic perspective on the fundamentals associated with credible communication. That vision and enhancement came as a result of Steven's search and ultimate connection with Dr Rebecca Weintraub, Clinical Professor of Communication and Director of the Master of Communication Management Program at the Annenberg School for Communication and Journalism at the University of Southern California. Nothing short of serendipity brought us together at a time in our lives when we both had stories to tell and experiences to share.

Rebecca was entering her final year at USC before retiring. Over those 21 years of teaching, speaking and writing, her thoughts about communication, perception, organizational culture and strategy had evolved and expanded. While she had been toying with the idea of a book – pretty much all academics do – she had never suited thought to action. When she met Steven, all of that changed. Both of us had finally found a partner!

And so we began.

During the one-year-plus writing process, even though we live and work less than 25 miles apart, due to the COVID-19 pandemic we met only once in person, on the eve of the formal lockdown. Writing and working via Zooms, Teams and Meets with many a Dropbox folder and files presented unique challenges, but also forced a deeper look at the essence of credible communication. Assumptions, expectations, conjectures and beliefs around all manner of communication that previously even we took for granted were turned on their end as people everywhere moved seemingly overnight into an almost universally digital and virtual world. Even as we wrote, we learned. Even as we learned, we researched. Even as we researched, our thoughts and perspectives expanded. You hold the result in your hand.

The remarkable and providential collaboration that became *InCredible Communication* is a timeless analysis of how and why we all need to be believed and trusted in our communication. This book offers readers an opportunity to deepen their understanding of the importance of cultivating credibility capital and understanding of how it integrates with others' perceptions of us. We hope it adds insight to your journey as writing it has done for ours.

Acknowledgements

We want to begin by expressing our deepest thanks and admiration to two women without whom this book would have been infinitely poorer. Dr Stefanie Demetriades was finishing her PhD at USC when she was recommended to be our research assistant. Thanks to Dr Patti Riley for that auspicious recommendation. Stefanie was part collaborator, part researcher, part editor and eventually, part friend during the writing process. Her meticulousness, knowledge of the field and good humour smoothed many a road bump. Stefi was never ruffled. Despite juggling many balls besides this book, she was the picture of calm and it was a picture we often needed! In addition to all of these contributions, Stefanie found us our illustrator, Alexis Demetriades. Yes, Alexis is her sister, but there was nothing nepotistic about the recommendation. Alexis combines immense artistic talent with a wry sense of humour that brought our notions to life. She even graciously tolerated our attempts at art direction. We are immensely grateful to these two amazing women and know our lives are richer for their being in them.

* * *

I wish to thank my mentor and *Media Savvy* former business partner Ramey Warren, who played a major role in bringing forth my skills to coach celebrities and executives to be their most genuine in every encounter. To John Bond, who provided support and counsel through the proposal and publishing process. To my parents, Jill and Joe, and sister Caren, whose love has always supported me and encouraged me to grow beyond my comfort zone. To my son William, who daily expands my mind to believe what is possible. And to my beloved Lois, for being the best wife, friend and shoulder anyone could ever dream of. To our two Curly Coated Retrievers, Cody and Cleo, who slept patiently at my feet for hundreds of hours when I'm sure they would rather have been outside running and playing.

And to my co-author on this journey, Rebecca Weintraub. Our finding each other was pure serendipity and the results of our collaboration brought this project to exciting new heights.

Steven Lewis
Pacific Palisades, CA

* * *

I wish to thank the people I worked with at Hughes Aircraft/ Electronics for being the crucible in which my perspective and perceptions of strategic and effective communication moved from theory to application. C. Richard Jones, Tony Iorillo, Malcolm Currie and C. Michael Armstrong gave me opportunities to experiment, fail occasionally and grow exponentially. To my colleagues at the USC Annenberg School of Communication, my deepest thanks for all you taught me as I watched and learned from you. You are the cutting edge of communication research and theory and make the world a better place with each article you write, every undergraduate you teach, Master's student you inspire and PhD student you mentor. I remain in awe of you all.

To my family, daughters-by-marriage, their husbands and my grandchildren, thank you for your encouragement and support during this year of creation. To my five siblings, their spouses, children and my 97-year-old-father, thank you for being willing to listen to my trials and tribulations during our weekly Covid Zoom calls. Thanks especially to my brother Howard Stolz for being such an appreciative reader of chapters in process. I owe you all a copy of the book! And, of course, to my loving, supportive and irreverent husband, Richard Loftus. His suggestions were not always the most appropriate, but they kept me in stitches when deadlines loomed large or writer's block set in. Without him, I might still be staring at a blank computer screen.

And last, but definitely not least, I must acknowledge my partner, my friend, my sounding board, my co-author Steven Lewis. Who knew what a lunch at USC could produce? I didn't then, but I certainly do now!

Rebecca Weintraub
Redondo Beach, CA

Introduction

Like most people, you may think about your communication skills only when you are giving a presentation. That's good, but it is not the way to become a successful and effective communicator. Today's highly connected world demands mastery of a myriad of communication skills and a deep understanding of how what we say and what we do is perceived. In this era of unfiltered information overload and increased ease of using remote communication technologies, clear messaging has never been more vital and personal credibility has never been more valuable.

InCredible Communication tackles the subject of how to thrive in organizations at a time when communication is increasingly complex and people's expectations are as high as they have ever been. If you found this book, you realize that sharpening your communication skills and understanding the communication culture of your workplace is essential to career success and advancement. Building your credibility capital is a key element to becoming a powerful communicator.

We've taken our combined experience of more than 75 years of real-world, evidence-based expertise in the art of effective business communication and assembled an easy-to-use approach to helping you build your communication mastery. Rebecca began her career at California Polytechnic State University, Pomona as a debate coach. She took that experience to Hughes Electronics, a major aerospace corporation. In both cases, she worked with engineering students and then engineers and scientists – people for whom communication is rarely a primary concern. As a Clinical Professor and now Emerita Clinical Professor at the University of Southern California Annenberg School for Communication and Journalism, she both coached executives and taught masters students in Communication

Management. Her perspectives on communication in the business world developed and evolved in the crucible of classroom discussions, student projects, academic research and its application in her consulting. Steven worked in entertainment in a variety of positions in which he worked with actors, producers, writers and executives as a publicist, consultant, coach, and mentor. But it was certainly his years as a television producer where he developed the ability to help people speak in clear, succinct sound bites to be used for broadcast. No matter the level of seniority we are working with, however, our core counselling and coaching mantra always remains the same: 'The more believable a communicator you are, the more successful you will be.' In this book you will find concepts, research, approaches and coaching to help you reach your full communication potential.

Each chapter begins with an illustration capturing the overall thrust of the chapter. These humorous and clever drawings are the work of a truly exceptional artist, Alexis Demetriades. While Alexis is a classically trained fine artist, she also has a wicked sense of humour that she made the most of in these cartoons. We believe her interpretations of the material in each chapter will make you laugh as well as give you something extra to think about.

The book offers *Self-Assessment, Foundational Concepts* and *Practical Advice* that will enable you to see the elements of communication in an entirely new way. Start with the Self-Assessment to gain insight into your communication approaches and qualities. The Foundational Concepts give you a rich understanding of how perception, context and credibility integrate to create formidable communication abilities. Practical Advice provides a deep look at communication in a variety of settings, including how to create and deliver a powerful presentation. Just as important, however, is understanding how to enhance your credibility in informal business communication situations, managing work relationships, using video conferencing, addressing conflict and understanding how you approach communication situations. These chapters include a short *Assessment Workbook* that examines your assessment results in the context of the chapters' content and helps the reader focus on their specific strengths and weaknesses.

We want to recognize Stefanie Demetriades, PhD who, in addition to being our research assistant and sounding board, was the primary architect of the Communication Assessment. Dr Demetriades' expertise in assessment, analysis and evaluation enabled the creation of a unique approach to enable an individual's deep understanding of their own communication. We know you will benefit from her insights as reflected in the Assessment itself.

Therefore, we strongly urge you to begin the book with the Assessment. This will help you understand yourself as a communicator in the broadest sense of the term. The assessment does not address skills but rather helps you understand your authentic communication self. Reviewing the *Assessment Workbook* will help you think about how the chapters' material can be integrated into your personal communication credibility capital and overall effectiveness. We encourage you to read all of the Workbook discussions – even those that do not apply to you. You will work with people whose communication qualities are different than yours. The more you understand about others, especially in how they relate to you, the more credible, the more versatile, the more effective and the more successful you will be.

Once you have taken the assessment and understand these elements of communication and where you fit in, you will want to read Part 2, Foundational Concepts. These are the basic building blocks of organizational and personal communication and provide a framework for the remainder of *InCredible Communication*. These concepts are grounded in both academic research and literature as well as our collective knowledge and understanding of what underlies business communication. These concepts are neither hard to understand nor complex and obtuse. Rather, they are fundamental to how people and communication interconnect. As you read them, you are likely to recognize elements that you already knew intrinsically but perhaps do not think about in the communication moment.

The third part of the book is practical advice, perspectives and coaching. You can read these in order or jump around to specific topics of interest or need. Perhaps you have a job interview coming up, so start with Chapter 15, Acing Interviews. If you have ongoing issues and disagreements with a colleague or colleagues, then take a look at Conflict, Chapter 11. Make sure, however, that you don't give short shrift to the *Assessment Workbooks* found at the end of these chapters. These should give you an individualized perspective on how the information contained in the chapter relates to you. This will help you develop your own personalized next steps.

Your communication credibility is inextricably woven into the fabric of who you are. The warp and woof of that fabric are experience and image with context and perception woven in for colour. Every presentation you make, every meeting you attend, every interview you give is another opportunity to demonstrate your credibility. In this book, we will reveal how you can become your best and most believable communicator self.

We wrote *InCredible Communication* to be a journey. *Your* journey of self-discovery. This is the best journey any of us can take. We wish you great success on what can be a truly fantastic voyage.

PART ONE

Self-Assessment

1

Your Communication Style Self-Assessment

By Stefanie Z. Demetriades

This book is intended to help you develop and hone your most credible – and therefore most powerful – communication skills. The most credible voice is an authentic one. So, rather than trying to force yourself awkwardly into a one-size-fits-all mould, it's worth spending some time figuring out what is authentic to your personal style of communication and where your inherent strengths and weaknesses lie.

Before you consider skipping this chapter because you're confident you already know your abilities, know that research consistently shows we are generally very poor judges of our own skills. Social psychologists have long documented people's tendency to overestimate their strengths and downplay their weaknesses. In fact, a now famous study by researchers David Dunning and Justin Kruger found that the less skilled a person is in a particular area, the more likely they are to believe they are in fact doing amazingly well.[1] The upshot of this 'Dunning–Kruger Effect' is that as long as you don't know what you don't know, there is likely to be a big gap between your instinctive judgement of your own abilities and the reality that everyone else sees. The good news is that with more objective insight, feedback and practice you can bridge that gap.

This assessment is the important first step in that process. It will help you identify your inherent communication style, preferences and habits. From there you can build on your strengths and guard against your shortfalls to become your own unique brand of an InCredible Communicator. To help you get the full benefit of these insights, at the end of most chapters will be topic-related recommendations that take into consideration what kind of communicator you are. Make sure you read through the recommendations that are offered for the other types of communicators. While these other categories might not apply to you, they do reflect the people you work alongside. Understanding how these people might act and react in various situations, will enable you to adapt in ways that increase your personal credibility capital with people who are different from you.

These questions are designed to home in specifically on how you communicate in professional and organizational settings. In truth, because communication style is innate to your individual style and tendencies, they probably remain a strong undercurrent in your personal life as well. Just as how you probably dress differently for

[1]Kruger, Justin & Dunning, David (1999), 'Unskilled and Unaware of It: How Difficulties in Recognizing One's Own Incompetence Lead to Inflated Self-Assessments', *Journal of Personality and Social Psychology*, 77: 1121–34.

the office than you do when going out with friends, however, chances are you also moderate your communication style at work – leaning into some instincts and resisting others. So, as you respond to these questions, have that professional framework in mind. Resist the temptation to look for a 'right' or more 'desirable' answer – there isn't one! Respond as honestly and intuitively as possible, without judgement. The more honest you are with your answers, the more valid and useful the results. You might find that there are some statements that don't directly apply to your day-to-day work life. Not to worry, these questions are designed to get at underlying preferences and tendencies in your communication rather than test specific practices. When in doubt, go with your first instinct.

You'll see that the questions below are divided into sections (A1, B1, etc.), with a score for each. Keep track of these section scores on a separate piece of paper (or take notes on your phone) for easy reference modelled after our suggested scoring sheet – you'll need them at the end of the questionnaire to calculate and interpret your results.

SELF-ASSESSMENT QUESTIONNAIRE

A1	Not at all like me	Somewhat like me	Mostly like me	Extremely like me
	1	2	3	4
How well would you say the following are true for you?				
i. People would describe me as very confident.				
ii. I have no problem arguing forcefully for my ideas, even if they are unpopular.				
iii. I believe complete honesty is the best policy, even if it ruffles a few feathers.				
iv. When starting a new conversation or topic, I skip chatting and jump straight into the main topic.				
Add response values to get your A1 Score:				

A2	Not at all like me	Somewhat like me	Mostly like me	Extremely like me
	1	2	3	4
How often would you say the following are true for you?				
i. When listening to someone speak, I often nod or say things like 'mmm', 'okay' and 'yes'.				
ii. I think I'm good at reading between the lines in what someone is saying.				
iii. I find it easy to see another person's perspective even if I don't share their opinion.				
iv. I believe misunderstandings are more likely to be the fault of the speaker rather than the listener.				
Add response values to get your A2 Score:				

A3	Not at all like me 1	Somewhat like me 2	Mostly like me 3	Extremely like me 4
How often would you say the following are true for you?				
i. People would probably describe me as detail-oriented.				
ii. I carefully proofread most emails and messages before sending.				
iii. I tend to be uncomfortable if I have to make a snap decision.				
iv. When speaking up in a meeting, I prefer to think through what I want to say in advance rather than jumping in spontaneously.				
Add response values to get your A3 Score:				

A4	Not at all like me 1	Somewhat like me 2	Mostly like me 3	Extremely like me 4
How often would you say the following are true for you?				
i. Given the choice, when making a presentation I would generally prefer to stay fairly still (for example, sitting or standing at a lectern) as I speak.				
ii. I tend to use simple, straightforward language.				
iii. People would probably say it's difficult to read my emotions.				
iv. I tend to find eye contact distracting when I am speaking and prefer to focus on my notes or slides.				
Add response values to get your A4 Score:				

A5	Not at all like me	Somewhat like me	Mostly like me	Extremely like me
	1	2	3	4
How often would you say the following are true for you?				
i. People often come to me with their problems.				
ii. I tend to be very aware of how others are feeling.				
iii. I often find it difficult to say 'no' to people.				
iv. When working in a team, I generally try to reach a consensus on a decision, even if that requires me to compromise.				
Add response values to get your A5 Score:				

B1	Not at all like me	Somewhat like me	Mostly like me	Extremely like me
	1	2	3	4
How often would you say the following are true for you?				
i. When sharing my ideas, I tend to use a lot of qualifying words and phrases like 'I think', 'maybe' and 'sort of'.				
ii. I worry that if I am too blunt with feedback, I will offend people.				
iii. People would probably describe me as tactful.				
iv. If I have to critique someone else's performance, I typically try to soften criticism by pairing negative feedback with praise.				
Add response values to get your B1 Score:				

B2	Not at all like me 1	Somewhat like me 2	Mostly like me 3	Extremely like me 4
How often would you say the following are true for you?				
i. When giving a presentation, I tend to be more focused on what I want to say than on how people are responding.				
ii. While on a conference call or video meeting, I tend to multitask to get other work done while I'm listening.				
iii. Once I have made up my mind, I am not usually interested in continuing to hear other perspectives.				
iv. I find that my mind often wanders when someone else is talking.				
Add response values to get your B2 Score:				

B3	Not at all like me 1	Somewhat like me 2	Mostly like me 3	Extremely like me 4
How often would you say the following are true for you?				
i. When meeting about a team project, I prefer to address topics that come up organically rather than follow an agenda.				
ii. I think best under pressure.				
iii. I enjoy unstructured brainstorming and tossing ideas around to solve a problem.				
iv. If a meeting or presentation isn't going as planned, I am generally confident in my ability to improvise and adapt.				
Add response values to get your B3 Score:				

B4	Not at all like me	Somewhat like me	Mostly like me	Extremely like me
	1	2	3	4
How often would you say the following are true for you?				
i. I tend to move my hands a lot when I speak.				
ii. I often use jokes or stories to make a point.				
iii. People would probably describe me as approachable.				
iv. I tend to convey a lot of feeling through my facial expressions when I speak.				
Add response values to get your B4 Score:				

B5	Not at all like me	Somewhat like me	Mostly like me	Extremely like me
	1	2	3	4
How often would you say the following are true for you?				
i. I generally prefer working individually over working in teams.				
ii. I am generally hesitant to share personal details or emotions with others.				
iii. If there is a disagreement in a meeting, I will argue for what I believe to be the right position, even if that upsets some people.				
iv. I believe the best ideas often come out of conflict.				
Add response values to get your B5 Score:				

ANSWER FORM

A1
1) _____
2) _____
3) _____
4) _____
*A1 Sum*_____

B1
1) _____
2) _____
3) _____
4) _____
*B1 Sum*_____

A2
1) _____
2) _____
3) _____
4) _____
*A2 Sum*_____

B2
1) _____
2) _____
3) _____
4) _____
*B2 Sum*_____

A3
1) _____
2) _____
3) _____
4) _____
*A3 Sum*_____

B3
1) _____
2) _____
3) _____
4) _____
*B3 Sum*_____

A4
1) _____
2) _____
3) _____
4) _____
*A4 Sum*_____

B4
1) _____
2) _____
3) _____
4) _____
*B4 Sum*_____

A5
1) _____
2) _____
3) _____
4) _____
A5 Sum _____

B5
1) _____
2) _____
3) _____
4) _____
*B5 Sum*_____

SCORING SHEET

Your Results

Dimension 1: How you Convey
Information

Median   15
(plus)   +
A1 sum   _____
Total   _____
(minus)   –
B1 sum   _____

Dimension 1
Score   _____

Dimension 2: How you Receive
Information

Median   15
(plus)   +
A2 sum   _____
Total   _____
(minus)   –
B2 sum   _____

Dimension 2
Score   _____

Dimension 3: How you Prepare
Information

Median   15
(plus)   +
A3 sum   _____

Total   _____
(minus)   –
B3 sum   _____

Dimension 3
Score   _____

Dimension 4: Your Communication
Personality

Median   15
(plus)   +
A4 sum   _____
Total   _____
(minus)   –
B4 sum   _____

Dimension 4
Score   _____

Dimension 5: How you Relate to
Others in Communication

Median   15
(plus)   +
A5 sum   _____
Total   _____
(minus)   –
B5 sum   _____

Dimension 5
Score   _____

INTERPRETING YOUR RESULTS

Using the scores tabulated for each of the previous sections, use the simple equations below to identify your communication style in five key dimensions. Mark where you fall on the ranges below for future reference.

Remember, these questions focus on an organizational setting. If you are surprised to find that your professional communication style is a significant departure from your personal communication style, take note! That's useful information to know because it tells you that first, you are good at adapting to different contexts – a valuable skill in itself – and second, that there may be opportunities to strategically let more of your personal style shine through in service to your authenticity and credibility.

Dimension 1: How you convey information
15 + A1 score – B1 score =

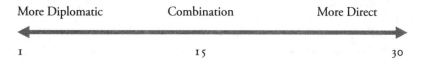

More Diplomatic	Combination	More Direct
1	15	30

If you boil down communication to the simplest terms as getting information from point A to point B, this dimension is about how straight a line that journey is for you as a communicator. More direct communicators take the express line; they prize efficiency and clarity in getting their point across. More diplomatic communicators, by contrast, prefer the scenic route; they would rather enjoy the environment and the company, even if it takes a little longer to get to the destination. Both routes can get you there, but the journey will be a little different, with different opportunities and pitfalls to look out for.

The more direct you are in conveying information, the more likely you are to be clear and assertive in your communication style: you know what you want to say and you go for it. This can be a powerful asset in effective communication, helping you avoid misunderstandings and ambiguity that might muddy your message. Used correctly, it can provide a good boost to your credibility capital, because people often appreciate and trust the candour and openness of highly direct communication. On the flip side, however, this penchant for directness can be so focused on getting *information* across that it sometimes comes at the expense of the *personal* elements at play. Too much directness can come off as arrogant, insensitive and alienating, not to mention rude.

If you are a more diplomatic communicator, efficiency is not the absolute priority for you; instead, you are more concerned with how others are responding to your message. You are more likely to ask people rather than tell them what to do. This can be a great strength when wielded effectively – especially when dealing with disagreements or delicate situations where you need to win people over to your side. Take this diplomatic tendency too far, however, and you risk coming off as indecisive or unreliable or just not very confident in yourself or your point of view.

Dimension 2: How you receive information
15 + A2 score – B2 score =

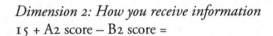

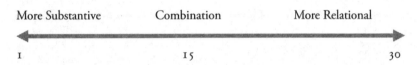

More Substantive	Combination	More Relational
1	15	30

If the first dimension is primarily about how you *convey* information, this one is about how you *receive* it. People who are on the more substantive side tend to pay most attention to the content of communication – the concrete pieces of information that are of use or interest. Those who are more on the relational side of the scale tend to be more aware of the people and environment they are in, picking up cues about how people are feeling or responding.

If you are more relational, you have the advantage of being able to take other people's perspectives into account in your communication. You are likely a natural at what you've probably heard of as 'active listening', engaging closely with what other people are saying to make sure you understand and process it, and you also have a good sense of whether or not your own messages are landing. In terms of credibility, this is a great tool to have because it helps you focus on perceptions, which is key to effective communication. A word of caution, though: tip the scales too far and you might find that you become your own worst enemy by compromising your goals or interests in the effort to appease others.

If you are more of a substantive communicator, your focus tends to be trained more inward than outward. You may find it difficult to pay attention when conversation shifts away from your primary interests and, in turn, you may not always realize when you are losing an audience yourself. You may well find yourself composing your responses while the other person is speaking. On the plus side, this ability to narrow your focus to the task at hand can be really useful in the right context and can help you keep your sights set firmly on what you want to achieve.

Dimension 3: How you prepare information
15 + A3 score − B3 score =

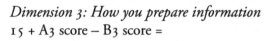

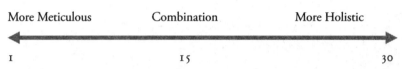

You can think about this dimension as relating to how you approach communication before you ever open your mouth to speak. What is your pre-communication process like? Do you shine in improvised, off-the-cuff contexts, or are you more comfortable when you have a plan?

If you are a more meticulous communicator, you likely fall into the latter category. Meticulous communicators value precision, organization and planning. You are thoughtful in how and when you speak and likely prefer to think ideas through on your own before sharing with others. This kind of attention to detail grants you the credibility of precision and reliability: people will listen to you because they trust you've done your homework. This is especially valuable in the professional workplace and, in fact, research shows that a detail- and goal-oriented approach is linked to strong job performance.[2] Watch out for blind spots that can come with a perfectionist streak, though: the details and planning that highly meticulous communicators love can make it more difficult to adapt to new contexts and situations that arise unexpectedly.

---

[2]Angelina R. Sutin et al., 'Personality and Career Success: Concurrent and Longitudinal Relations,' *European Journal of Personality* 23, no. 2 (March 1, 2009): 71–84, https://doi .org/10.1002/per.704

If you are more holistic, that doesn't mean you are careless; it means you are more likely to enjoy big-picture thinking and embrace flexibility in your communication. Unconstrained by a firm adherence to detail and planning, you are able to think on your feet. You probably tend to think aloud and freely share ideas without prejudging them. As a matter of credibility, that flexibility and authenticity can be very effective in winning people over. Without sufficient structure or discipline, however, this flexible, big-picture perspective can put you on the path to inconsistency and an over-confidence in your ability to wing it.

Dimension 4: Your communication personality
15 + A4 score − B4 score =

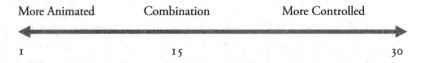

More Animated	Combination	More Controlled
1	15	30

Whereas the previous dimensions are all primarily about how you relate to *information*, this one is all about *style*. This is the unique personality you bring to your communication through your use of voice, language and physicality.

If you are a more animated communicator, you have an expressive, engaging way of speaking that naturally draws people in. Animated communicators tend to use their whole body when they speak, conveying a lot of feeling and information through facial expressions and gestures as well as through their voice. Here, there's a lot to use to your credibility advantage: interpersonal and non-verbal communication expert Judee Burgoon, for instance, has conducted studies demonstrating that speakers with vocal and physical expressiveness tend to be perceived as more relatable and persuasive.[3] There is such a thing as too much of a good thing, though: especially when it doesn't suit the context, an animated style run rampant can

[3]Burgoon, Judee K. et al. (1 September 1985), 'Effects of Gaze on Hiring, Credibility, Attraction and Relational Message Interpretation', *Journal of Nonverbal Behaviour* 9, No. 3: 133–46, https://doi.org/10.1007/BF01000735

become more of a performance and can undercut the substance of what you're trying to communicate.

People who are more controlled in their communication style tend to focus more on the content of their communication and keep their feelings closer to the chest. If this is you, you may be more comfortable in a quieter, more subdued manner of speaking than your more emotive counterparts. You are likely to prefer smaller meetings in which to present your thoughts. There are challenges to this to be sure: you may find it more difficult to hold an audience's attention for extended periods of time, especially in bigger groups. You could end up underutilizing some really powerful persuasive tools that draw on emotion and storytelling. But a restrained communication style has its unique advantages as well and can lend instrumental authority and calm to your credibility capital.

Dimension 5: How you relate to others in communication
15 + A5 score – B5 score =

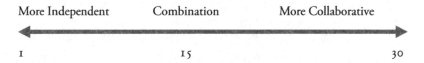

More Independent	Combination	More Collaborative
1	15	30

The final dimension has to do with your interpersonal style and reflects how you approach and prioritize relationships with others in your communication. So, is your communication geared more towards creating connections or achieving outcomes?

If you are a more collaborative communicator, you are conscious of how the way you communicate with someone will affect your interactions going forward. You think of communication in the context of longer-term goals and relationships and probably strive for consensus wherever possible. This orientation is often associated with empathy and perspective-taking, you are probably perceived as warm and open. This emphasis on developing relationships benefits your credibility, providing a well of goodwill you can effectively draw on when you need people on your side. Left unchecked, however, an overwhelming focus on relatability can slip into unproductive people-pleasing and risk-avoidance at the expense of your own interests.

If you are more of an independent communicator, you may still value relationships, but your first priority is reaching your more tangible goals in a given context. You are less averse to conflict and more willing to go against the grain of popular opinion. You have the advantage of independence, which can be invaluable in situations where you need to defend your ideas and interests. As always, though, be conscious of letting this tendency dominate completely. People may interpret your approach as a desire to drive conflict, an arena you are more comfortable with than most. Extreme independence may lead to others seeing you as aggressive, aloof or rigid – none of which helps your credibility capital.

APPLYING YOUR RESULTS

As you consider these communication dimensions and how your style fits within them, remember the results of this assessment reflect your communication comfort zone – but that doesn't mean they are immovable or deterministic. Think of them as orienting guideposts, pointing out areas in your natural communication style to be conscious of as you develop your skills. In some communication contexts, your inherent tendencies will work to your advantage; in others, they might present challenges that you have to consciously counteract. Versatility, adaptability and flexibility are critical credibility capital success factors. To navigate this, at the end of each chapter you will find a series of tailored tips designed to help you focus on how to improve your skills based on the kind of communicator you are.

COMMUNICATION DIMENSIONS AT A GLANCE

How you *convey* information

Direct
Make the most of:
efficiency, clarity, openness
Watch out for:
alienating others, aggressiveness

Diplomatic
Make the most of:
sensitivity, diplomacy
Watch out for:
not clearly expressing or advocating
for yourself

How you *receive* information

Substantive
Make the most of:
clarity, focus
Watch out for:
missing cues and opportunities for
engagement

Relational
Make the most of:
perspective taking, empathy
Watch out for:
undercutting your own authority

How you *prepare* information

Meticulous
Make the most of:
precision, organization
Watch out for:
missing the forest for the trees, rigidity

Holistic
Make the most of:
flexibility, big picture thinking
Watch out for:
inconsistency, winging it

Your communication *personality*

Animated
Make the most of:
engaging verbal style and body
language
Watch out for:
style over substance, scene-stealing

Controlled
Make the most of:
authority, composure
Watch out for:
tone, losing audience attention

How you relate to others

Collaborative
Make the most of:
personal warmth, openness
Watch out for:
people-pleasing

Independent
Make the most of:
independence, consistency
Watch out for:
aloofness, anxiety

PART TWO

Foundational Concepts

2

Credibility Capital

In 1972, US President Richard Nixon began his second term, having won more than 60 per cent of the vote. By August 1974, he had resigned amid what we've all come to know as the Watergate Scandal. In the intervening two years Nixon's involvement in the scandal and its cover-up became more and more apparent and more and more damning. Nixon repeatedly claimed his innocence, but to little effect.

After denials of and subsequent revelations of damning recorded conversations, Nixon's cover-up lost him the trust of the country. He had spent all of his credibility capital on perpetual lies and his presidency never recovered.

Credibility capital can be amassed and leveraged, but it can also be squandered. Understanding how to build it, how to protect it and how to use it is fundamental to becoming an InCredible Communicator. The concept of credibility capital, while not easily entered into a spreadsheet, is a tangible human asset often worth more than dollars, euros, pounds or yuan.

Credibility capital is made up of your amassed trust, believability, history, integrity and veracity. It's what others believe is your competency and accuracy. It is what Aristotle called ethos. While you do the work to build your credibility capital like entries on a resume or CV, it actually only lives in the perceptions of your stakeholders. Your factual history provides a baseline by which others may judge you, but true credibility capital requires frequently demonstrating that you are listening to your stakeholders and taking what you hear into consideration. Communication researchers McCroskey and Young suggest two overriding elements to credibility – competence and character.[1]

However you wish to define credibility, always remember that your credibility is determined by what others think it is, not what YOU think it is. Where you do have control, however, is in how you build and protect your credibility capital. Paying attention to what you do, how you do it and how others see it will enable you to do just that.

WHAT YOU DO

Think of your credibility capital as being similar to that QuickBooks ledger for your 'human' business. Like most things of value in any venture, credibility capital is built over time. Each time you do what you say you will do, you add to your assets column. When you betray others' trust, however, you add to your liability column. Increasing credibility capital

[1]McCroskey, James C. & Young, Thomas J. (1 March 1981), 'Ethos and Credibility: The Construct and Its Measurement after Three Decades', *Central States Speech Journal* 32, No. 1: 24–34, https://doi.org/10.1080/10510978109368075

requires attention and care. You don't build it overnight, but rather over and over and over time. While it takes time to build credibility capital, it can take but an instant to damage or lose it.

People are always observing and making judgements about others. Sometimes we do this consciously and are aware of these impressions. Often, though, we don't pay attention to the details, just to our unconscious conclusions. If someone routinely fails to return an email or a phone call in what we think is a timely manner, for example, we begin to think of them as unreliable. If asked, we might not be able to give the specifics, but will remain firm in our perceptions and that will affect our relationship and behaviour with them.

People interpret actions – but they also interpret non-action. What you do has consequences, both good and bad. What you *don't* do often has its own consequences and these are almost always bad. When you do not come through on a project as promised, your credibility suffers. No matter the reason, no matter how justifiable in your mind, in others' minds it is likely to be a credibility demerit. Sometimes described as 'walking the talk', your words and your actions have to match.

When actions do not match the words, the actions speak much more loudly. Promises not kept are credibility capital killers.

HOW YOU DO IT

Your competency is a big part of your credibility capital. It may not seem to be a major part of any specific communication event, but in reality, it colours every recommendation you make. We can look at competency in two buckets, skills and qualities. The former are learned, the latter inherent, but both are integral to building credibility capital.

Just to be hired requires having the skills needed for the job. This kind of competency addresses what you have to do to be successful in your career. Being able to use a software program, write code, manage a project, sell a product or pen a press release are all skills. They are learnable. Being competent means consistently having and using the skills to produce the expected results.

More important, however, are the qualities that go into perceived credibility. Skills are learned and they vary by career and position and years on the job. Qualities are intrinsic to us as individuals, they are part of our nature. They show up no matter our jobs, careers, organizations and industries. Some are universal, others less so, but the qualities linked to competencies are critical credibility capital building blocks. They encompass how you do what you do.

The qualities of competency will vary a bit, to be sure. An ability to work well in a team may be important in jobs that are project based and require input and involvement of many people. In jobs that work more on an individual level, teamwork may be neither expected nor desired. In this kind of job, however, an ability to self-motivate is likely to be crucial. In both cases, however, not exhibiting these assumed qualities will hurt your credibility because there's a disconnect between expectation and outcome.

Other qualities that go into competence are more apparent. A record of diffidence in taking a stand may leave people feeling that you do not have the confidence or courage of your convictions, begging the question of why you should be trusted. Being willing to take that stand, having the courage of your principles, defending your position will give them assurance you are a person of conviction. Even if they disagree, you will have built your competence credibility capital. We admire people who speak their mind – appropriately.

Lissa Freed, Global Head of Human Resources for Universal Filmed Entertainment Group, puts it this way: 'I encourage authenticity and continuity of messaging. I believe the more open and transparent leaders are the better and more conversational approach is most effective. Those who are willing to be vulnerable and show compassion while creating a vision and being decisive are most successful in my experience.'

Developing a reputation of being responsible in how you do the work you do is critical, no matter what the job. Holding yourself accountable, not making excuses when something goes wrong, being a problem solver all go towards building credibility capital. In short, demonstrating that you can be counted on matters ... a lot.

HOW OTHERS SEE YOU

Real credibility capital is built little by little over time. People begin to trust you know what you are talking about. They learn you can be counted upon. They trust that when you say something is true, it is indeed true.

Credibility is contextual in that it varies in relation to the situation and the people in it.[2] You may have deep credibility capital in one arena but very little in another. This relates to how people assess your competence or trustworthiness or goodwill as it pertains to a specific event. You have to project your competency so that you affect their perceptions of your credibility. It is a dynamic and organic process, it is not static.

Communication competency is integral to credibility. In fact, a study by Coqual (formerly the Center for Talent Innovation) found that 'projecting credibility' and 'communicating effectively' were among the most important areas of mastery required among global executives.[3] We would argue that these two qualities are in reality two sides of the same coin: your credibility is presented through your communication. You build your credibility through your communication as well. This doesn't mean that you have to be a particular kind of communicator to have credibility, but it does mean that your credibility capital will go farther when you master the power of your communication skills and make the most of your inherent strengths to project the best authentic version of yourself for a given context.

Think about two doctors. Both may have the same education and the same numbers of years performing a surgery in a particular specialty, yet one is the must-see expert in their field and the other, while equally competent, is not sought as highly. The reason? One has mastered empathetic communication – better known as 'bedside

[2]McCroskey, James C. & Teven, Jason J. (March 1999), 'Goodwill: A Reexamination of the Construct and Its Measurement', *Communication Monographs* 66, No. 1: 90–103, https://doi.org/10.1080/03637759909376464; McCroskey, James C. & Young, Thomas J. 'Ethos and Credibility' (date?); Holmes, William T. & Parker, Michele A. (January 2017), 'Communication: Empirically Testing Behavioural Integrity and Credibility as Antecedents for the Effective Implementation of Motivating Language', *International Journal of Business Communication* 54, No. 1: 70–82, https://doi.org/10.1177/2329488416675450
[3]Sylvia Ann Hewlett, Noni Allwodd, Karen Sumberg and Sandra Scharf with Christina Fargnoli, 2020, Coqual Research Report, *Cracking the Code: Executive Presence and Multicultural Professionals*.

manner' – and the other simply presents the facts of the case and the possible remedies. While medical schools teach basic communication skills and how to explain medical procedures, the credibility capital of the doctor who takes the time to go beyond the facts and speaks to patients and their families with sensitivity will always bank the most credibility capital.

Credibility capital, like most components of first impressions, is ours to lose. People start out wanting to believe what we represent. The more we can take stock of who we are and what we offer, the more aware we are of the credibility capital we control and have at our disposal. How you do this and how you build on that credibility capital with your communication competence is what this book is all about.

3

Communication Culture

We've all heard companies touting their cultures or talking about changing their culture or planning on merging two cultures after an acquisition. Culture just permeates an organization.

Walk into Zappos' offices and you know this is not the culture of a bank or a law office. The American online shoe and clothing retailer has no individual offices – even for the CEO. Staff work in cubicles that are brightly decorated with all manner of posters, handwritten signs and flags. It feels fun. You just know this is not an ordinary or usual corporate culture. After all, has anyone described a law office culture as fun? Face it, we don't want our lawyers to be fun. We want them to be serious, focused experts. The often sombre, heavily wooded spaces lined with law books reflect a culture designed to give clients confidence their cases, and their fates, are in good hands.

Of course, culture is more than office space, although that can be a major indicator of how an organization's culture functions. Scholars define organization culture as consisting 'of the sum total of shared values, symbols, meanings, beliefs, assumptions and expectations that organize and integrate a group of people who work together. As such, corporate culture essentially consists of the set of presuppositions that make up a worldview ... and the product of that worldview, such as values, stories, myths, artifacts or rituals.'[1]

Ed Schein of MIT's Sloan School of Management offers some useful clues you can use to figure out a company's culture. Schein suggests looking at things that are *visible*, artifacts; things that are *promoted*, espoused values; and things that are *unspoken and unconscious*, underlying assumptions.[2]

Artifacts vary in type and some are more obvious than others, but in general, they are observable. Some artifacts you identify immediately, such as dress codes, even those that are not stated. You figure out pretty quickly when business formal, suits, ties, pantsuits, dresses are virtually required. Other artifacts are a bit more complicated to identify quickly. Companies have traditions that are part of the culture, but they are rarely codified. Social events for anniversaries or new product launches are deeply embedded in the culture but you won't find them in any company manual. Meetings are deeply imbued with a communication culture, including punctuality. In some organizations, arriving on

[1]Sriramesh, K., Grunig, J. & Buffington, J. (1992), 'Corporate Culture and Public Relations', in *Excellence in Public Relations and Communications Management: Contributions to Effective Organizations*, ed. James E. Grunig, Routledge, 577–96.
[2]Schein, Edgar H. (2009), *The Corporate Culture Survival Guide*, 2nd ed., J-B Warren Bennis Series ; v.158, San Francisco, California: Jossey-Bass.

time finds you in an empty room. In others, you will find yourself without a seat and the discussion in full swing. One of the more interesting artifacts resides in an organization's use of slides in presentations. In the US military, slides are filled with data, charts, graphs and a lot of words. There is an expectation of thoroughness that equates quantity with quality. Microsoft, on the other hand, expects few words on a slide and a more creative graphic design. Interpose one for other at your peril!

Espoused values are pretty much what they sound like: what organizations say they are about. Look at a company's website or walk its halls and often you will see a prettily formatted sheet of vision, mission and values. Organizations equate these values with their culture. They point to them in discussions with investors. Companies tout them to recruits, pointing out what a good place theirs will be to work. CEOs reference them as they answer questions at town hall meetings with employees. All too often, however, the artifacts of an organization conflict with that which is espoused. A company may have directors for diversity and inclusion yet have senior executive ranks that don't reflect this value. Managers tout their open-door policy and willingness for people to drop in to chat. In reality, the doorway might as well be made of glass because people learn quickly not to walk through it.

Underlying assumptions are not observable and they are not spoken about. These are, as Schein suggests, perceptions, thoughts and feelings that drive the values and help create the artifacts. These are the most powerful elements of culture and communication and the least understood or acknowledged. These days, companies talk about their ethics, but truly ethical organizations have this commitment deeply ingrained in their DNA. Principles of fairness, merit and equality are baked in and unfortunately, so too are their opposites. Morals and scruples, and the lack thereof, are embedded in the culture. What makes these assumptions so difficult to identify is that perceptions, thoughts and feelings do not live in a company – organizations have no perceptions, but their people do.

An organization's culture is an amalgam of what is embedded in its people. You learn the communication cultural assumptions beneath the words from being in the organization, sometimes by osmosis and sometimes by painful trial and error. These underlying assumptions are revealed only by communication – in words, actions and images. Often, it is not in the words where true underlying assumptions are revealed but in action and non-action. What people do communicates, but what they don't do communicates even louder and is remembered far longer. Often it is what is missing, what isn't said, done or shown that reveals the real underlying assumptions of an organization. An organization that does not share a lot of information with employees reveals that they do not value employees beyond the narrow scope of the work they do. They may speak differently, but the fact they keep material about the company's business close to the organizational chest means that employees are considered mere cogs in the wheels rather than important elements of the engine driving company growth and success.

Many an employee has been heard to mutter about the company 'walking the talk', the implication being that what is said and what is done do not match. Nothing impacts company culture more than inauthenticity, so beware of cultural inconsistencies.

These inconsistencies have an impact on credibility. A CEO of a multi-billion-dollar company was proud of his willingness to hear opposing views and encouraged his executive team to 'push back'. His team quickly learned to ignore this encouragement because the CEO showed no interest in their input. Their comments were ignored at best and ridiculed at worst. The irony of the situation is that the CEO genuinely believed he was welcoming input – but he could not be blamed if so much of what he received was poor! He clearly believed that any ideas or perspectives not his own were of little use.

Communication culture is a powerful force in shaping expectations and interpretations of messages within an organization. Research on the topic suggests that communication is culture and culture is communication. Much of what we point to as culture boils down to communication and interpretation, whether it is action, behaviour or talk.[3] Understanding an organization's communication culture is key to being a credible and effective communicator within it.

[3]Eisenberg, Eric & Riley, Patricia (2001), 'Organizational Culture', in *The New Handbook of Organizational Communication: Advances in Theory, Research, and Methods*, Thousand Oaks, California: SAGE Publications, Inc., 291–322.

Misanalysing seemingly simple communication cultural situations can get you off to a bad start. A renowned consultant was invited to speak to the top 50 executives at a Fortune 100 company's quarterly off-site meeting. He was given 30 minutes. Assuming the time frame was a mere suggestion, he did not pay attention to the time limit either when preparing or during his talk, ignoring time signals. He went 25 minutes over time. The group had become antsy and frustrated with this violation of their norms and asked no questions. As he was walking out, the next person to speak was heard to say, 'Oh great, the idiot goes over time and now I have only ten minutes!' Worse, the executive who had lobbied for and invited the highly-paid speaker was called on the carpet by the CEO, who held him responsible for the fiasco. No surprise that the consultant was never invited back and the executive had a big demerit next to his name.

Leadership is not immune to the problems that arise from cultural mismatch. Heather Rim, Chief Marketing Officer at OPTIV, put it this way: 'When you look at the critical first few months for a new leader, a big predictor of their success is the way in which they embrace the company culture. As communicators, it's our job to help executives learn the lay of the cultural land, but it is nearly impossible for a leader to be successful in the long run when there is a big cultural disconnect. Inevitably, engagement drops and performance suffers. Unfortunately, more often than not, a bad cultural fit results in a parting of the ways between the leader and the company.' In short, often leaders believe they can remake the organization's culture in their own image. This is like teaching the proverbial pig to sing – it can't be done, and it annoys the pig!

Culture is the context in which the organization functions. Communication is the medium that enables the functioning. If you were to go into a new organization and you wanted to understand its culture, you would do well, then, to begin by looking at how the organization communicates. We suggest you begin by looking at the language people use, the symbols employed, the stories told and the practices in place.

The language used in organizations reflects its culture. Words have meaning and that meaning is heavily contextual. The dictionary may define employees as people who are paid to do work, but in actual fact, there are many different contextual meanings. The term can mean staff or labourers or bodies on the payroll. Companies with a participative culture will often refer to employees as 'associates', thinking the term indicates they value employees more as engaged partners than subordinates. Employees can be self-managed work teams who have control over their work, schedule and budget. They may be seen as people who do the tasks assigned to them without having to worry about extraneous facts, figures or decisions. It all depends on the cultural contexts which give the term its meaning.

If you want to be a credible communicator in an organization – as an employee or associate, a supplier or a consultant, you will need to understand their meaning of terms. Use language as the company does and you will be more likely to connect with the people with whom you are communicating and working.

If you are speaking to an organization with which you are unfamiliar, you will, of course, have done your homework to learn all you can about them. Pay attention to what you see when you arrive. Remember, things and symbols communicate. Does the lobby function as a gateway that requires you to sign in with security? Is there a formal receptionist who must announce you? What is the conference room or auditorium design? Can you tell who the leader is just by the seating? All of these symbols reflect the communication culture. You may find yourself needing to adapt if what you see is at odds with what you expected.

Language and symbols are clearly essential elements of company culture. There is one more component that complements them and that is the stories organizations tell. Stories are an important binder of the cultural threads. They explain the present in the context of the past and become predictors of the future. To you as a communicator, they are shortcuts to interpretation. It may be tempting, if you are an outsider, to refer to organization stories. Do so judiciously. You want to be acknowledging, but not come across as obsequious or worse, as if you are one of them!

Among the most common are stories about company founders. Particularly prominent in tech, these stories bring to the fore the power of near-mythical accomplishments of invention, creativity and innovation. Everyone at Apple, and consumers everywhere, knows the story of how Steve Jobs and Steve Wozniak began the experiment that has become a technology powerhouse. In her bestselling autobiography, *Tough Choices: A Memoir*, former Hewlett-Packard (HP) CEO Carly Fiorina tells a story about overcoming cultural issues.[4] Dissatisfied with how things were progressing, one of her early moves was to create a document of expectations called 'Rules of the Garage'. The Rules referred to the iconic garage where Bill Hewlett and David Packard founded what would become HP and the cultural basics they instilled in their company. Fiorina used the founders' story to help guide HP into what she saw as its future. Pay attention to the stories – they matter.

ELEMENTS OF COMMUNICATION CULTURE

Clearly, understanding the communication culture of an organization is critical to being a successful, and credible, communicator within it. The question then is how to do this. It can be helpful in deciphering the communication cultural codes if we think about how we can classify the communication culture. There are four elements to be considered: transparency of communication, impenetrability of communication, controlling communication and integrating communication. These elements intertwine and provide a tool for assessing the communication culture of an organization.

Transparency

There is a lot of lip service paid to the idea of transparent communication but in truth, this can be hard to come by. Lars Christensen and George Cheney suggest that transparent communication involves 'insight, clarity, accountability and participation' and that it demands total accuracy.[5] Transparency suggests trust, that is participants in the culture can rest assured that what they hear and see is all there is to see and hear. There is nothing hidden, nothing withheld, nothing unaccounted for. Complete informational transparency may

---

[4]Fiorina, Carly. *Tough Choices: A Memoir*. New York: Portfolio, 2007. Print. Turabian (6th ed.)

[5]Christensen, Lars & Cheney, George. (2015). 'Peering into Transparency: Challenging Ideals, Proxies, and Organizational Practices.' *Communication Theory*. 25. 10.1111/comt.12052.

be difficult to provide, especially in publicly-held companies who function under governmental rules and regulations, or in privately-held companies working to keep their secrets from competitors. Being transparent about these limits can actually create trust in the organization's commitment to transparency.

Transparency is intimately linked to trust; stakeholders must trust that what the organization is saying is true and the organization must trust that stakeholders will use the information in ways supportive of the organization's goals. Brad Rawlins observed that for an organization to be truly transparent in its communication it must meet three criteria: '[the] information ... is truthful, substantial, and useful; [there is] participation of stakeholders in identifying the information they need; and objective, balanced reporting of an organization's activities and policies that holds the organization accountable.' [6]

Transparency is not binary but rather a continuum of communication cultural norms. A company may choose to be extremely open with employees on the costs and options of benefits and explain in excruciating detail why they made decisions to curtail or cut certain healthcare options, but not share information on pay. Their trust quotient can be increased, however, despite this lack of openness if they are transparent in their reasoning. Trust can be gained, ironically, when people feel they are not being lied to, even if information is being withheld.

Perception has a great deal to do with transparency. Face it, transparency is never an objective fact – it isn't something we can see or touch. Rather, it is something we believe, based on the information we receive. Organizational communication transparency is found in stakeholder's perception. If they believe there is open, honest, transparent communication, then there is. But woe betide the organization if that perception, and that trust, evaporates.

Impenetrability
You can think of communication in an organization as running through a kind of mesh. The more open the mesh, the more

---

[6]Rawlins, Brad. (2008). Measuring the relationship between organizational transparency and employee trust. *Public Relations Journal*. 2.

communication flows. The finer the organizational communication mesh, the more impenetrable the flow. Communication flows through an organization downwards, from the top of the organization to the bottom; upwards, rarer but bottom up; horizontal, lateral between people and equal units; diagonal, up or down but not in the stated hierarchy; and external, to and from those outside of the organization proper.

While a great deal of these communication flows are formal messaging, perhaps the more essential element of these flows are conversations. James Taylor and Elizabeth Van Every suggest that conversation is ubiquitous in organizational communication dimensions, whether the informality of hall talk or 'the more arranged and circumscribed encounters of meetings, interviews, appraisals, [and] briefings'.[7] The more impenetrable an organization's communication flow, the more likely information will stay within small groupings of people. This will show up in the kinds of topics people are willing to discuss when they meet at the proverbial water cooler as well as the types of issues discussed in meetings, briefings and the like.

Organizations are created by communication but also by the lack thereof. Impenetrable flows may exist formally in the sense that certain topics and the information pertaining to them are discussed only at certain levels of the organizations or in particular venues. They also exist informally in the unspoken and unacknowledged but understood and followed constraints. Embedded deep within the communication culture, these interrupted flows can be difficult to discern. Ignoring them, however, is deadly.

Restrictive
An organization with a highly restrictive communication culture is one that formally and consciously limits, obstructs, restrains and prevents communication from being shared. This is more than just interrupting flow, as in impenetrable communication cultures. Rather, a restrictive culture welcomes dialogue and information from only a

---

[7]Taylor, James R. & Van Every, Elizabeth J. (1999), *The Emergent Organization: Communication As Its Site and Surface*, London: Routledge.

trusted few. A military or governmental organization is likely to have a somewhat restrictive culture.

Organizations such as these view information as power and view decision making as the realm of a chosen few. How they are chosen might change by management level or function, but they see no advantage, indeed a disadvantage, in seeking input from those outside their ranks. Restrictive communication cultures are wary of outsiders and see competitive boogeymen in every virtual nook and cranny. In a world of instantaneous and catholic communication, where bits and pieces of information – true or false – find their way onto the Web, this concern is certainly not unreasonable. The challenge for these organizations is in balancing the need to protect with the need to inform and be informed.

Integrative
An integrative communication culture looks to incorporate information, ideas, suggestions and approaches from throughout the organization. Sometimes thought of as an emergent organizational perspective, this kind of culture is a system which views the whole by far greater than the sum of its parts. Certainly in their early days, start-ups develop an integrative culture. The challenge is to keep that kind of culture as they grow.

Integrative communication is multi-dimensional. Information, conversation, perspectives flow in a kind of Brownian motion,[8] unrestrained by policies, procedures, mores or expectations. While this may look undisciplined to an outsider, within the organization it is usually seen as a competitive advantage because innovative ideas know no hierarchy. Conversely, however, this can result in information overload and mayhem as emails have long strings of cc'd addresses, meeting minutes are sent out to everyone and decisions await multiple rounds of feedback and additions.

In an effective integrative communication culture there are expectations and approaches designed to manage but not eliminate

[8]Brownian motion, or pedesis, is the random motion of particles suspended in a fluid resulting from their collision with the fast-moving molecules in the fluid (Wikipedia).

the disruption. Much of the responsibility for this, as would be expected, falls on the individual rather than the organization. Eschewing rules and pronouncements, an integrative organization onboards new employees in a buddy-like system, where people learn by observing, as well as the occasional major misstep. Key to the success in this kind of communication approach is a high tolerance for risk and error. Ambiguity enables employees to think way outside of their boxes. To work, however, this requires a willingness to forgive, forget and learn from errors in the long term.

An integrative communication culture will be more difficult in an industry grounded in rules and regulations, such as banking, aerospace and finance. It will be much more of an advantage in a start-up or technology company. As a company grows, however, fostering an integrative culture becomes more of a challenge. Eventually, the law of big has to be faced. As organizations grow, risk grows exponentially. The more people in an organization, the more likelihood of a communication free-for-all. This is why so many institutions that began with a highly integrative communication culture become more restrictive as they grow.

Looking at an organization in terms of these factors can help you identify the communication culture and norms. There are eight communication culture classifications:

1. Collaborative
2. Committee
3. Controlling
4. Callous
5. Cautious
6. Clinical
7. Collegial
8. Condescending

The following chart indicates where these classifications fall in the quadrants created by the four elements. Where does your organization place?

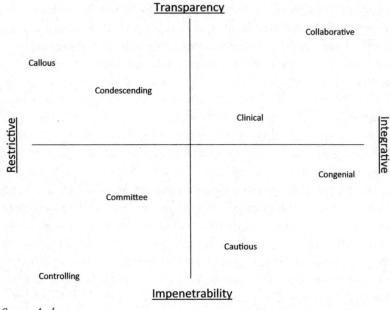

Source: Authors

COLLABORATIVE COMMUNICATION CULTURE

High transparency and high integrative
Communication in a collaborative communication culture is open and focused on sharing information as deeply into the organization as possible. While there may always be some things that cannot be widely shared, especially in a publicly-held company subject to Securities and Exchange Commission (SEC) Rules and Regulations or relating to research and development, a collaborative environment focuses on what can be communicated rather than what cannot.

Collaborative companies strive for a highly integrative and participative communication culture. Transparency works in both directions, not just broadcast out but receiving in. The goal is to share information such that it results in engagement and participation across the organization. Employees and other key stakeholders are invited to react, respond, inquire and interact with both the information and the company. This culture does not merely pay lip service to input, it seeks it out and encourages dialogue.

A collaborative communication culture values input and is open to pushback from within. Welcoming opposing positions, encouraging debate and discussion, these organizations assume that a wide range of information and ideas are the best cauldron for good decisions.

COMMITTEE COMMUNICATION CULTURE

Moderate impenetrability and moderate restrictive
Communication in a committee communication culture is generally focused on need to know. Information is doled out by category or project or subgroup. This culture views information as a resource, much like technology or equipment. In the same way that not all employees or departments require the same kinds of computers or software, a committee culture views information as linked to the project or product.

Committee organizations expect information involvement from recipients only so far as it is required for the work to be done. These cultures expect information to be siloed and not shared beyond the subgroup unless it is necessary for the work to be done. Feedback on the information shared is expected only to ensure accuracy and usefulness.

Information in these kinds of organizations is kept at the highest levels of management. While understanding that having the right information enables the right decisions, it is up to the leadership to determine just what constitutes the right information. This culture protects its information but not at the price of results.

CONTROLLING COMMUNICATION CULTURE

High Restrictive, High Impenetrability
A controlling communication culture views its information as part of its competitive advantage. It is to be safeguarded and shared only to those who are part of the inner sanctum and who can be trusted to protect it at all costs. Communication in a culture such as this is top down and narrow in scope. Their communication philosophy means that employees do not need to worry about the company beyond their own job or unit.

Control of communication in this culture flows two ways. New ideas, innovations and perspectives from rank-and-file employees are stifled and then die. Employees learn early that communicating up is ignored at best, unwelcome at worst.

CALLOUS COMMUNICATION CULTURE

High Restrictive, Moderate Transparency
Sheer decibel count can often identify a callous communication culture – this is the culture of yellers. Emotions run high in these organizations, where reactions are rarely filtered, primarily negative ones. Insensitive to others' feelings, people express outrage, frustration and anger in often insensitive, and sometimes cruel, ways.

The communication in a callous culture is often perceived by the organization's members as open and honest. Critiques are straightforward with little or no emotional withholding. A missed deadline might result in a berating of the offending parties and the get-well plan an unyielding set of expectations with little or no explanation expected or offered. Highly creative and demanding people waste little time in what they perceive as the niceties of communication. Straightforward information is what they want and need.

For the uninitiated, this culture can inflict hurt feelings at best and real psychological damage at worst. The leaders of the organization, who almost always shape these cultures, are likely to give complainers short shrift. If this communication culture is too hot, better that employees learn early to get out of the organizational kitchen.

CAUTIOUS COMMUNICATION CULTURE

Low Impenetrable, Moderate Integrative
A cautious communication culture is a bit like the phrase physicians use: first, do no harm. This is the culture of check, recheck and double-check information, briefings, spreadsheets, email, pretty much anything shared with anyone else. Errors are deadly in these communication cultures, sometimes because of the nature of the work performed and sometimes because of the nature of the people.

These are the organizations in which work is organized around check sheets. That can be a very good thing! Certainly, none of us would want to fly on a plane for which the pilot had not done a pre-flight check. You would not want a Certified Public Accountant to send to the Revenue/IRS their first draft of your tax return. You would expect a nurse to check carefully that you are who you are supposed to be and that the IV drip is giving you the drugs you are supposed to receive. There are very real concerns for exactness in these examples.

Not all cautious communication cultures grow out of these kinds of life or death – audit or refund – situations. Cautious communication cultures can be the result of dealing with a mercurial leader. Unlike a callous culture, however, a cautious culture seeks out information from throughout the organization. In this sense it is integrative rather than restrictive but it is also somewhat impenetrable in that conversation and discussions are moderated by concerns, or maybe even fear, of reactions. The desire to avoid an eruption is what drives the check-recheck response in these companies. A mercurial leader models behaviour that others will emulate, even when it has a deleterious effect on candid conversation.

A cautious communication culture comes about because of the fear of failure. That fear can relate to the disastrous consequences of bad decision-making, or because of the fear of an unpleasant and unnerving reaction from someone in power. In both cases, the cautious communication culture reflects an attempt to control results not by withholding information but rather by ensuring that every i is dotted, every t is crossed and all is perfect.

CLINICAL COMMUNICATION CULTURE

Low Transparency, Low Integrative
A clinical communication culture is one that attempts to take as much human emotion and predilection out of the organization's communicative processes. While the organization is willing to share information and seek input to a degree, the focus is on data. Emotions cloud data interpretation and too much input impedes efficiency.

These organizations exist for their data. They make decisions based on evidence, attempting to remove as much subjectivity from the process as possible. Often found in medical or scientific organizations, the clinical communication culture is based on a perspective that there are quantifiable, proven solutions. While striving to be objective, there is also a recognition that new knowledge is to be sought and new insights applied. These, however, are expected to be the result of reason and evidence rather than intuition and instinct.

A clinical communication culture can seem cold and distant to an outside observer. Often an erroneous interpretation, this communication culture can exhibit passion and excitement, but is usually associated with data or a new proven discovery. In short, it is focused on discovering and applying new knowledge.

CONGENIAL COMMUNICATION CULTURE

Low Impenetrable, Moderate Integrative
A congenial communication culture is an agreeable culture. Compatibility and amiability are valued. People are given the opportunity to participate in the implementation of decisions and so information is shared but parcelled out carefully. The goal is to have people understand and be comfortable with decisions but not necessarily be included in the process. Questioning decisions is discouraged but accepted when expressed in an understated and affable manner.

This is a genial culture in which debate is accepted but only as long as it is done in an agreeable and genial approach. This culture values humour as long as it is not hostile. A social and amicable culture, it is very conflict avoidant. Issues are hashed out in private or not addressed at all. Once a decision is made, opposition is discouraged.

A congenial communication culture is a nice culture. Meetings are pleasant. This lack of discord, however, can be a negative side effect of the niceness. When opposing perspectives are discouraged, especially in the decision-making process, valuable insights are lost. Clashes can be uncomfortable and this culture tends to value consistency over controversy.

CONDESCENDING COMMUNICATION CULTURE

Moderate Restrictive, Low Transparency

A condescending communication culture views information as something not everyone in the organization needs. Information is shared in small bits of often inconsequential communication bites.

Sometimes haughty, often patronizing, management and leadership in a condescending communication culture believe that most stakeholders neither need nor want more than is doled out. This is a small picture culture in which the major communication assumptions are grounded in the perspective that people's need for information is focused on the work they do, not the company as a whole. In this case, the perspective is the whole is pretty much separate from its parts.

The kinds and quality of the media used in a condescending communication culture are simple, visual and general. This is a culture that makes use of town halls but with questions collected in advance. Dialogue is discouraged, not so much because leadership fears pushback but rather because they don't think there is any value to be gained.

A condescending culture is one of layers, of information haves and have nots. Leadership will deign to explain but in the main the overall attitude is disdainful of the idea that employees have a need to know much beyond their own jobs.

To be credible is to be able to speak into the organization's communication culture. To do so effectively requires doing your research in advance. Ask questions of what is expected from a speaker. Know how decisions are made. Understand how they value information and data. When you are speaking, use your senses and your intuition to read the room. Pay attention! This enables you to give a speech to a group of executives showing you understand them. You know what kind of information they want and what they can do with it. You use language as they do. You couch new concepts in language they value. You speak with them, not at or to them. And in that case, you are likely to be invited back.

4

Perception is Reality

The phrase 'perception is reality' is so seemingly overused as to be almost meaningless. Yet, in its very triteness lies its truth. Our reality – what we hold to be true – lies in how we perceive the world. This concept of perception and its relationship to reality is key to understanding the nature of communication. Communication is fundamentally an interpretive process; the intent of your message only gets you halfway there, it's the perception of your message that gives it meaning.

The simplest dictionary definition of communication is a 'process by which information is exchanged between individuals through a common system of symbols, signs or behaviour'.[1] Basically, we send and receive signals – verbal and non-verbal – that are then interpreted as messages. In effective communication, these signals and meanings line up nicely so that they are similarly interpreted by those who will receive and act on them. Thus, the signal of a red traffic light becomes a message that we should apply our brakes and stop the car. We trust that everyone in the cars around us on city streets perceives the red light to mean stop the car. It would be a very unsafe world if we did not share that belief and suit it to action.

Sounds pretty straightforward, doesn't it? Alas, as much as we would all like communication to be straightforward and simple, it is not. Why? Because humans are not straightforward and simple. We are complex, filled with individual experiences and idiosyncratic understandings of the world which affect how we think, how we analyse, how we interact and, yes, how we receive and act upon communication from others.

The theorist Professor Karl Weick studied organizations and the process of organizing. One of his key tenets, which is applicable here, is the notion of sensemaking. Weick suggested, 'The basic idea of sensemaking is that reality is an ongoing accomplishment that emerges from efforts to create order and make retrospective sense of what occurs.'[2] At the heart of this kind of sensemaking is recognizing that communication goes through multiple layers of interpretation.

Let's start with language. The words we choose are never neutral: they always carry meaning beyond their literal definitions and those meanings don't just reflect an objective truth, they construct a shared reality. That's why companies sometimes change the language they use to describe the people who work there to reflect or create a different relationship and a culture of inclusion, clarity and respect. Thus 'employees' become 'associates', 'supervisors'

[1]https://www.merriam-webster.com/dictionary/communication
[2]Weick, Karl E. (December 1993), 'The Collapse of Sensemaking in Organizations: The Mann Gulch Disaster', *Administrative Science Quarterly* 38, No. 4: 628, https://doi.org /10.2307/2393339

become 'coaches', 'departments' become 'teams' and so on. While there is a lot more to creating a new workplace culture than the words used to describe it, the words themselves can begin to foster a new perception. That same principle applies just as well to the personal level as it does at the organizational level. For example, Rebecca has three stepdaughters who were young adults when she married their father, so she really did not parent them. She is not a stepmother in the sense that other families might use the term but she disliked referring to them as her husband's daughters because she has a loving, direct relationship with them, so she coined the term 'daughters by marriage' to describe that relationship. That wording clarified and reinforced the nature and nuance of her relationship with the mothers of her grandchildren, and created a shared language and meaning that binds them together.

Words are tricky things, though, because their meanings are never fully set. Meanings shift over time; words that were commonplace or innocuous in the past, for example, become taboo in the present. Individuals' words themselves also often have conflicting meanings and connotations that can land very differently depending on who is on the receiving end. And that variability is at the heart of the challenge: our interpretations of communication signals, even beyond the content, are highly personal and contextual. These individual perceptions are created out of our experiences, our values and our judgements. Much of this is shared with others, but not all and not all the time. Value judgements – what we hold to be good – are not necessarily universal. These are the stuff out of which political arguments are created, after all: the role of government in society, what constitutes the good of the individual versus the good of the group, are not provable, physical facts, they are interpretations, perceptions and judgements.

Interpretation is also subject to the preconceptions associated with whoever is attempting to create that understanding. We all come to the table with preconceived credibility issues and very little time to convince others of the sincerity of our positions. For better or worse, we're hardwired to make quick judgements about others: in fact, psychological research shows that people start to develop firm impressions of traits like trustworthiness, likability and competence within just a fraction of a second of meeting someone.[3] That is not by any means to say that everyone starts from a place of hostility or suspicion, but nobody enters into any communication context with a clean slate on either side and preexisting beliefs, implicit assumptions or past interactions or experiences with someone all inevitably impact their credibility on any subject to the positive, the negative or shades in-between. When leaders are truly trying to make an impact and communicate effectively, they know that what they say will already be coloured by every other conversation they've had on similar subjects. To complicate matters further, the colouring also will come from conversations of leaders from the past. There is no rewind and erasing of past messaging. The conversation takes place in whatever relationship of trust, or a lack of it, already exists. It's all 'stored' in our brains and subconsciously filters our perceptions. The very fact that much of what goes into creating our perceptions happens at a non-conscious level just adds to the complexity when we try to develop shared meaning.

Try this. Think about a dog. A real dog. How big is it? What colour? What breed? Then imagine someone tells you, 'A strange dog jumped on me today.' If your image of a dog was, say, a Great Dane, you might imagine the person was practically mowed down by this big animal. But if your image was a Toy Poodle, it is an entirely different image. That's because there is no such thing as 'a dog'. There are types of dogs, sizes of dogs, breeds of dogs and they run the gamut from friendly to fierce, playful to protective, tiny to tremendous. The image in your mind when you hear the word 'dog' is based on your personal experience and cultural context. You may also interpret that message as ominous or joyful based on your perception of that image. And therein lies the challenge. There is no single right way to interpret the word 'dog' and so the mere exchange of information is not necessarily going to create a shared understanding of what that information means.

[3]Willis, Janine & Todorov, Alexander (1 July 2006), 'First Impressions: Making Up Your Mind After a 100-Ms Exposure to a Face', *Psychological Science* 17, No. 7: 592–98, https://doi.org/10.1111/j.1467-9280.2006.01750.x

People also use the past to make sense of the present and to predict the future. It's a good thing we do this or we would all still be touching a hot pan and burning ourselves. We learn more than just physical lessons from our past. We learn values. We learn ideals. We learn how decisions drive actions which drive results or do not. And so we take those past lessons and use them to guide our actions today to create a desired future. We make sense out of what we have experienced yesterday to determine what can and should be created for tomorrow.

Communication is fundamental to the concept of the future. Take a moment to think about the future. What time period comes to mind? One year? Five years? Retirement? Truth be told, the future is actually NOW, even though we do not think of it that way. The future tends to start where our sense of now ends. If a meeting, a holiday, a dinner is in our planner, we have made it real and it feels like now. This is what vision is – the ability to literally see in your mind's eye something in the future. It has no mass to it beyond our conception. But that conception creates an ability to act to bring it to literal reality. That conception has its beginning in language in our description of it. Once we have put language around the concept and given it mass – even if only in our words, minds and planners – it begins to have a sense of reality for us.

When the coronavirus hit the world in early 2020 it lobbed a virtual atomic bomb into pretty much everyone's vision for what that year would be like. Our visions of what could and would be created in those 12 months went up in smoke. Plans were derailed, businesses closed, governments stymied, classes moved online and life became one long Zoom meeting. Add to this the fact that there was seeming randomness in who became most ill and uncertainty associated with when things would go back to 'normal' and it is no wonder that our views of the future became one big empty calendar. This may be the first time in modern human history that such a massive undoing of expectations of the future occurred.

It isn't just individuals who work to create visions of the future. Organizations do it as well. This is because, as Karl Weick observed, a critical element in organizational development is a social process. This social process is an intricate dance of cues and feedback, action and consequences that happens at the individual, group and organizational levels.

With all of these caveats and challenges, the creation of shared meaning remains the ultimate goal of effective communication. Out of our process of creating meaning comes a rich tapestry of perceptions. The woof and warp of this tapestry are actions and concepts. Together, over time, they intermingle to become the bedrock of what we hold to be true – true yesterday, true now and true tomorrow. The fundamental issue, however, is that the very individual nature of these perceptions means that each of us has a slightly – or very – different perception of reality.

When we turn our attention to communication and being an effective and credible communicator, we plow headfirst into this wall of perception tapestries. For we have our own perception tapestry that is guiding us in what we think is the best course of action, the right way to spend scarce resources, the most promising and innovative approaches to problems. What we tend to do then is work to turn our perceptions into our audience's and stakeholders' reality. Our communication strategy, then, is to create charts and arguments and graphs and endeavour to be as persuasive as possible to ensure that the audience shares our perceptions such that those become their reality. It is the right goal, but the wrong strategy.

It is the wrong strategy because it begins with the wrong premise. We are, in this case, being self-centric. Our arguments are those that are persuasive to us, that match our set of perceptions. When we are speaking to audiences or stakeholders, however, OUR perceptions become less relevant than we would like because we move into the interpretive world of THEIR perceptions and reality. This does not negate efforts to influence those perceptions in our favour, but it does give us an important starting place. We have to understand not just what their perceptions are but to realize that these are their views of what is true and real. Thus, their perceptions become our reality, not the other way around. We see this in brands as well. A brand isn't what controllers of the brand say it is, it's what others say the brand means to them. The operational lesson is that their perceptions trump our rightness. What they believe to be true is more important than what we hold or say to be true. Within our audience and stakeholder perceptions lie the strategic underpinning in how best to approach the communication goal.

In short, it isn't about what we find persuasive, it is what THEY will find persuasive.

Fundamental to achieving the desired results, then, is understanding the 'what' and 'how' of stakeholders' perceptions. The term stakeholder, rather than audience, can be a powerful shift of perception for the communicator because we are allowing for the understanding of agendas that colour those realities. When we describe the people or group we are working to persuade as an audience, that creates a certain relationship. By its very definition, the word 'audience' classifies them as passive recipients of communication. The term itself does not countenance dialogue or active engagement. We expect audiences will understand the points made and move to a different point of view, the one we are advocating. It becomes even more difficult when audiences have minimal mechanisms available to give feedback.

As we engage an audience, we may see them nod their heads. That is usually seen as a positive by a speaker because we tend to interpret a nod as a signal of approval. Of course, we don't know exactly what they are agreeing with – assuming that the nod was truly a positive signal. While there can be contextual indications of their intent, all we know with objective certainty is that their necks work such that they can move it up and down. The reason this matters is we really do not know what their nod means. Which part of our talk are they reacting to and what in their past experiences is triggering an almost involuntary acknowledgment and/or acceptance of what we are saying? Is the meaning of that statement or statements what we intended? Do we have shared meaning or not? And there, as they say, is the rub.

A fundamental underpinning to successful and credible communication, then, is understanding that stakeholders' perceptions really need to become our reality as well. Our understanding of what their perceptions are, why they have them, what created them becomes the linchpin to creating successful communication. With this understanding comes the need to see receivers as engaged and interactive, with perspectives of their own. The term 'stakeholder' helps to create this because the term refers to people, groups or entities with a stake in what we are trying to achieve – their unspoken agendas and how their world may be impacted. The word 'stakeholder' versus the word 'audience' literally changes the nature of the relationship between speakers and receivers. It becomes shared rather than a one-way process. Audiences are passive. These instances are not dialogic. A sermon, a play, a political speech are all intended to be one-way communication. Stakeholders, on the other hand are engaged with the issue, the strategy, the presenter. Remembering that stakeholder perceptions are our reality is a critical first analytical step towards achieving successful communication. Understanding why they hold those perceptions is second. And third, and most important, is to ensure that our messages resonate with these stakeholders because of, not despite, their perceptions.

An important part of that process is understanding the resistance points and adapting your communication to get around them. When faced with a set of perspectives, arguments, observations that differ from their own perceptions and agendas, all too often people's initial tendency is to reject the premise, the evidence and the examples. Human nature is to hold onto our own perceptions first and foremost. This may be easiest to understand if we look at how this concept fits into our personal lives. Your spouse or roommate may have a penchant for assigning certain spaces in the refrigerator for certain items. This is their definition of refrigerator goodness. You, on the other hand, figure that if the refrigerator doors close, then all is well. Your spouse explains over and over why their way is better using arguments that are *persuasive to them*. Trouble is, those arguments are just not enough to make you want to change your behaviour. You remain happy in your position that all that is needed for refrigerator goodness is that the doors close and everything remains cold.

Of course, people can be persuaded to change their minds, but it is neither fast nor simple, so a communicator has to acknowledge that the recipients of the messages are not necessarily open or ready to receive our thoughtful and compelling approach to a problem. Often, the negative reaction is not triggered by the recommendation itself but the experiences with seemingly similar initiatives in the past. The comments are universal – 'We tried that before and it never worked', 'You don't understand what our customers really want', 'How is this going to be different than the past seven quality improvement campaigns?' The more we understand what is driving their interpretations of what they are hearing today, the better our chances of persuading them to believe that something different and good is attainable.

Having a sense of what stakeholders hope to hear as opposed to what they are likely to hear is the first step in changing their perceptions and achieving a shared reality. It is rare that stakeholders are going to hear what they want to hear – after all, if that were the case successful communication would be far easier and far more consistent. The more we understand what is driving them, the better able we are to create communication that will resonate with them.

Sometimes speakers are sanguine in their certainty that their stakeholders will change their beliefs. This confidence, often misplaced, stems from a conviction the stakeholders just know the speaker wouldn't lie to them and is telling them the truth. Therefore, if it is the truth, it must also be compelling. Truth in this instance can be considered what they consider to be fact, their honest opinion based on experience or belief systems, or what they believe to be moral. So, assuming that others are likely to believe and agree with us is a nice fiction, but it is just that, a fiction. The very concept of truth in this instance is relative because truth stems from belief, and beliefs are individual and wide-ranging. Even what some might consider factual, scientific truth about, say, climate change is not a belief universally shared. This is a hard notion for many people who think about Truth with a capital T. Without getting into a philosophical discussion, suffice it to say that an understanding of stakeholders' truths, what they believe is true, is fundamental to producing successful communication. If you do not understand where their beliefs, perspectives, perceptions and truths are grounded, you have a very slim chance of moving them in your point of view direction.

While the concept of 'perception is reality' might create a fear that communication and shared meaning are fundamentally difficult and maybe unattainable, it's actually at the core of what we need to know to become better communicators. If our communication is stakeholder-centric, that is focused on the people with whom we want to create shared meaning, rather than self-centric, what we believe to be true and persuasive, we have a significantly better chance of success. Our ability to step out of ourselves and see and hear through the minds of others is the first step towards realigning how we achieve a shared perception, which in the end is the ultimate goal.

5

It's All About Context

Context is everything! Admittedly a HUGE statement, but not overly hyped. Just ask any comedian bemoaning the reaction to a set that 'killed' one night and 'bombed' the next. Comedy can often be a painfully accurate barometer of context. To get the desired effect from comedy requires more than a passive understanding of the common references, comforts and insecurities of an audience. When these understandings are overlooked, it can certainly be painful for the speaker, but often equally uncomfortable for the audience. Context shifts meaning because it shifts the interpretation of meaning. It forces us to consider both the controllable and uncontrollable factors colouring our communication. Completely successful communication can only be achieved when presented within the framework of agreed upon context. Without such acceptance and understanding of context, it would be like a field of football players trying to score goals with their own made-up sets of rules. That is not to say context in and of itself should rule our messaging, but if we ignore it, we risk our ability to achieve our communication mission. Quite literally, different contexts can change the meaning of what is being communicated.

In its most basic structure, we can think of three distinct but interacting components or kinds of context: Physical, Cultural and Situational. Understanding these contexts enables us to adapt and adjust to the specific circumstances.

PHYSICAL CONTEXT

Probably the simplest contextual element to address, physical context is composed of a wide range of environmental elements from geographic location to venue size and capacity in which we will speak. Construction and formatting of our message may be heavily influenced by the size of the room: for instance, the set-up, anticipated distractions and time constraints of a formal talk or presentation will be very different to those of, say, a cocktail party or business lunch. Understanding the physical context not only allows you to mentally frame your communication, it can also take some of the pressure off your anticipated encounters.

Mastering physical culture is about familiarity. The most at-ease speakers take advantage of the chance to walk the room in advance. This is far more than just knowing where you will stand, checking out a podium height, acoustics or evaluating the scope of your ability to make eye contact with your audience, all of which are important. Being able to see and digest a space can calm your brain as you envision yourself presenting in the space. Some people even do this to take some of the anxiety out of a first date. They may choose to scope out a restaurant or bar in advance or they pick a familiar spot to minimize the impact of the unpredictable.

Any unprepared encounter with a physical space creates the potential for distractions that can take you off your game so checking out the space is important. However, don't just assume that because you know the physical layout means you are done with physical context analysis. There is one more important step and that is to envision yourself within it. You will need to think about your communication style, approach and skills. In this book we offer numerous ways to adapt to and embrace even the most daunting challenges presented in the physical context of a communication event. Challenges to be overcome are addressed in Chapter 10 for Meetings; Chapter 14 for Zoom communications; and Chapter 16 in dealing with High Anxiety.

Even if you are fortunate enough to be communicating from the comfort of your home, with just a video camera on, chances are you're not going to be completely at ease with the physical context. In recent years we have begun to realize there are no entirely 'safe' zones for communication. For many, this realization came in 2020 when the COVID-19 pandemic hit, work moved to the home and face-to-face communication moved to video. Even when the pandemic is just a distant memory, the flexibility, ease and cost savings of remote interaction will still result in people communicating virtually. So, just hoping the Zoom call or the Microsoft Teams or the Webex meeting will go away forever is fantasy.[1]

For some, maybe many, speaking to a camera with a bunch of faces in boxes can be more stressful than looking at a sea of hundreds in an auditorium. With a video camera you are basically always on, even when someone else is speaking or questions are being asked. It takes away a lot of the control of the physical context. Virtual or in person, physical context is an important element of communication success. Taking control of a video meeting's physical context is more about eliminating self-destructive unforced errors than managing a room. The physical context of the video box is a restrictive prison, missing

---

[1]Susan Lund, Anu Madgavkar, James Manyika, Sven Smit, Kweilin Ellingrud, Mary Meaney and Olivia Robinson, (2021). *The Future of Work After Covid-19*, McKinsey Global Initiative Report.

only the vertical bars to complete the image. Many of your gestures are unseen, visual aids are reduced to screen shares. There is hope, however. Your 'Get Out of Jail Free' card is your eye contact with the camera and therefore your audience. You will take back control of the physical context by maintaining your focus on the lens and the quality of the audio. That is not to say that an occasional glance at your audience is a bad thing, but such practice is often distracting in a video set up and threatens to take you off of your game.

CULTURAL CONTEXT

In 1981, German philosopher Jürgen Habermas wrote a two-volume book entitled *The Theory of Communicative Action*.[2] Thematically, Habermas looked to tie language and expression into a concept of reason related to societal norms. The notion that communication is more connected to cultural touch points rather than individual expression is the foundation of cultural context. Cultural context is vast. It emerges organically from a variety of factors such as region of the country, economic level, education and the concomitant societal norms and values. We are more the product than the creator of the cultural context in which we live. If effective communication is rooted in mutual understanding, no matter where that understanding comes from, then the basic premise of cultural context is important to take to heart. Making a communication connection is far easier when there is common ground on which we can build shared meaning. And while we all come to every situation with sets of different life circumstances, a shared cultural context can take away a major stumbling block to achieving that meeting of the minds.

Think about that stand-up comic again. Getting a laugh, seemingly simple, is actually quite complex. We have all seen jokes fall flat – professionally or personally. To work, the premise of a joke requires setting up a series of accepted and understood circumstances and then pulling the rug out from under that premise. Just how far that rug can be yanked is a reflection of the accepted cultural context, a delicate dance that is completely dependent upon the successful reading of

[2]Habermas, J. (1984). *The Theory of Communicative Action*. Boston: Beacon Press.

both the cultural context of the situation and the receivers. That's why our comedian was a hit in Boston and a flop in Columbus. The expression, 'Will it play in Peoria?' actually has its roots in Vaudeville from the late 1880s well into the twentieth century. At the time it came to be thought of as a litmus test of how entertainment would be accepted across the country. (It was later appropriated by Richard Nixon's Assistant for Domestic Affairs, John Ehrlichman, who often posed the same question while counselling the President on the public's potential reaction to controversial pronouncements.) 'Peoria' was thought of as a yardstick of contextual acceptance across society. Without that acceptance, there can be no successful communication.

So where does that leave us in trying to crack the code of cultural context? The first step is acknowledgement and understanding it as both a challenge and opportunity. This is more than simply knowing your audience. Cultural context goes to the framing of what that audience expects and needs to hear within their societal points of reference. What are the foundations you have to lay to create a common language? Even if your message is outside of their realm of immediate cultural understanding, there are basic dots that have to be connected. Even as early as the 1800s, sociologist George Herbert Mead explained, 'the individual mind can exist only in relation to other minds with shared meanings'.[3]

We will further discuss shared meaning in other parts of this book, such as our Chapter 17 about Putting it all Together, but for the sake of our explanation of cultural context, here we will focus on the core values and beliefs rooted in shared understanding. These are foundational interpretations that are ingrained in us from a time we were very young, impressionable creatures. They are a set of mores that comprise our social DNA and influence how and why we believe to be universal truths. Pretty heady stuff for a discussion of communication, but it is the framework from which we make thousands of instantaneous decisions about how to react to and process all communication.

Historically, much of cultural context was rooted in regional homogeneity. When communication technology consisted of telegraph and telephone, cultural context remained in close geographic quarters.

---

[3]Mead, George Herbert & Miller, David L. (1982), *The Individual and the Social Self: Unpublished Work of George Herbert Mead*, Chicago: University of Chicago Press.

That changed with mass media. First with television and movies and then with the explosion of social media, regional cultural differences became smaller and smaller. Scholars Joshua Meyrowitz and John Maguire suggest that despite the US being home to its most diverse population ever, mass media wears away at 'both old local identities and traditional notions of national identity by blending them into one communication system'.[4]

Understanding mutually accepted cultural context is in the best interest of advertisers who are trying to reach the biggest audience possible with a single message. Before technology allowed for targeting and digital marketing, a Super Bowl ad was the gold standard of mass messaging in the US. But that level of dollars expended, and potential audience reach, could only work if there was an understood shared context. In the US it was generally accepted that the more homogenous the audience, the greater chance for success. In the early years of three or four network television this was achievable. Yes, there was always programming that had stronger regional appeal in certain states or cities, but on the whole, message penetration and broad acceptance worked.

Today the dollars for ads on the Super Bowl might be as high or even higher, but they require a never before seen level of follow-up and intense online marketing to make that investment worthwhile. Why? Because cultural diversity requires a new sophistication of understanding cultural context and what pushes those emotional/transactional buttons.

In our own communication practices, we don't have huge advance teams of researchers and analysts at our disposal to evaluate cultural context, but we do have the ability to assess the accepted norms and tailor our messaging appropriately. Cultural context in the business realm is multidimensional. People bring into the workplace the cultural context of the state, region, country, but when they enter the organization, that cultural context becomes paramount. An organization's cultural context exists in how its members communicate, what they communicate, where they communicate and why they communicate. It goes beyond that, however. There can be sub-cultural contexts within divisions or units or departments. The sales department

---

[4]Meyrowitz, Joshua & Maguire, John (July 1993), 'Media, Place, and Multiculturalism', *Society* 30, No. 5: 41–48, https://doi.org/10.1007/BF02700289

may well suggest a different cultural context than R&D or engineering or finance. A sales presentation is likely to use slides much differently than finance or engineering. Their expectations of level of detail, use of charts and graphs, even the number of words must be met, or you run the risk of a missed connection. Miss these important cues at your peril. The more you understand context and what that says about what motivates and satisfies your audience, the more engaged your listener will be and the more credibility you will retain.

SITUATIONAL CONTEXT

The first time Steven worked with a young actress destined to be a mega star he was tasked with training her for a promotional appearance at the world's largest Comic and Science Fiction Convention. This actress had just been announced to play the part of a beloved literary character whose popularity was taking the world by storm and whose story was about to become one of the most successful theatrical series in history.

The casting of this lead character had been the subject of months of speculation. In the books, she was described as having olive skin, straight black hair and grey eyes. When the official casting was announced, the only photos widely seen on the internet were of a blonde, blue-eyed, fair-skinned actress who looked absolutely nothing like what fans envisioned. As she was not widely known as an accomplished actress, she immediately became the social media target of a barrage of angry messages and hurtful feelings. The fans seemed to blame this betrayal on the actress personally.

In preparing her for what she felt was going to be a terrifying experience, Steven advised that her opening line to the thousands of attendees should be simply, 'To be honest, after reading the books myself, I wouldn't have cast me either.' Not particularly funny or clever, but it worked. It diffused the moment by sharing her understanding of their emotions. As she is a genuinely sensitive and empathetic person, this direct acknowledgement, made in the proper context, came across authentically and she won hearts, and ultimately praise, for her performance.

If we think of cultural context as the deeply rooted tapestry from which we unconsciously make evaluations of messaging, then situational context is the other side of the coin. Situational context is everything happening in the moment that might impact your ability to connect. News events, stock market activity, Twitter posts, hot personalities, recent innovations and trends, for instance, can give you immediate points of reference with those who you are trying to connect. Additionally, and potentially more importantly, they can give you background on what may be important to your audience.

Whether speaking within your own organization or pitching to a new one, you want to understand the situational stressors facing the company. If you find yourself making a sales presentation to a company that has just announced a reduction in force and associated cost cutting, you face a much more difficult situational context than speaking to a company who just posted record profits. You would want to build your credibility by acknowledging the situation in the former and showing how what you are selling will help them control costs. In the latter, you would want to understand the relationship between the piece of the organization to which you are speaking and those record profits. You might not need to reference it, but it will give you situational contextual understanding of the issues facing your audience.

Sometimes, situational context is all about the person rather than events outside. In the case of a personality readying for a promotional tour, situational context is all too often about something negative they did and the story that emerged about it. Depending on the perceived severity of the offence, the best way to address the narrative is probably head-on. That can be said of any rumour or gossip that emerges ahead of your planned encounter even if you are not a celebrity. The veritable 'elephant in the room' is called that for just such a reason – it cannot be ignored, nor should it be. Acknowledging a potential distraction avoids it taking over your ability to communicate anything else. Such a visible disconnect with reality is difficult to recover from.

While there is always a need to be responsive to a challenging environment, not all situational culture is negative. There may have just been reports of a company's quarterly success or a story in the news of someone attaining a monumental physical feat or the grand opening of an attraction or venue in the community. Acknowledging joyous events in the moment allows you to tap into the positive feelings associated with that event. If you are an outsider, it also provides an example of your efforts to embrace something of which your audience is proud.

Situational context can also allow you to make something of an opportune moment. It could be an unanticipated presentation derailment or an unscripted reaction to a set of circumstances from which you can emerge as a memorable star. This kind of immediate situational context requires being aware, agile and adaptable. Taking advantage of these times with a self-deprecating bit of humour or a quick save after a stumble can actually be a once-in-a-lifetime chance to make an indelible impression. Situational context requires being and staying in the moment.

Context is the grand lens and filter through which we see and hear everything. Reading context can be the difference between success and failure in communication. Abandon the notion of controlling context and embrace the concept that it is more important to understand it and use it to your advantage. Such is the foundation for *InCredible Communication* that allows you to frame any message with respect for your audience and an appreciation of what is meaningful to them. Within the proper context, anything is possible.

PART THREE

Practical Advice – Becoming an InCredible Communicator

6

Brand You

The idea of people as brands has long circulated among life coaches and marketing professionals as a novel way of defining who we are and making it easier for others to understand our perspectives and motivations. The benefits of instantly attributing identifiable signals to who we are just seemed obvious. It turns out the notion of comparing ourselves to a bottle of Heinz ketchup isn't always that appealing. Memories of *Mad Men*-like sixties ad campaigns with comparisons to the ubiquitous 'Brand X' have made personal brand acceptance difficult.

The truth is this is all semantics. People are brands. You may not think of yourself that way because you think of brands as things, not people. If you look at it a bit differently, people as individuals with different and diverse talents, perspectives, histories and societal filters that make them unique ... well then, the concept of branding becomes applicable. The concept of personal branding actually brings together the time-tested analysis and understanding of consumer-based loyalty and combines them with elements of an individual's authentic personality. The result can be a brand that's personal, influential and embodies the clarity of who you are, what you stand for and what your messages mean.

Brand Guru Marty Neumeier defined brand in his book *The Dictionary of Brands* as 'a person's perception of a product, service, experience or organization'.[1] Now that's more than the average condiment! The right product brand can conjure up memories of spending time with your family, long walks on the beach, being rescued from a tricky situation or just opening a cherished birthday present. If the term 'brand' makes you feel too much like a de-humanized product, then just think of it as the key for others to unlocking what it is about you that will let them see what you can contribute to their lives. Try taking away the word 'brand' and just replace it with what a brand really is – meaning. In a cut-to-the-chase concept – your brand is what do you want to *mean* to others? – David Ogilvy, the father of modern advertising, went even further to define a brand as 'the intangible sum of a product's attributes'.[2]

Replace the word 'product' with the word 'person' and you begin to see that looking at yourself as a brand is not such a terrible thing after all. Face it, whether you choose to cultivate it or not, you are a brand.

[1]Neumeier, Marty, *The Dictionary of Brand*, https://www.slideshare.net/liquidagency/the-dictionary-of-brand-by-marty-neumeier
[2]Ogilvy, David (1983), *Ogilvy on Advertising*, ed. Christopher Fagg, New York: Crown Publishers.

You have the power to control what is tangible about your brand as perceived by peers, staff, friends and stakeholders.

At its simplest, a brand is a promise. A promise of meaning. It is the promise of what you mean to all those who interact with you. It is your meaning that shapes your relationships with them and is based on all of your unique, value-creating characteristics. Basically, your personal brand is the way you are perceived by those who experience you.

Think of all the first impressions of people you have amassed over your lifetime. People with whom you have immediate affinity and those to whom you just couldn't warm up. You interpreted a myriad of signals that became your unconscious view of their brands. Over time, it is very possible your initial reactions will change after you have spent more time together. We all know, don't we, how long-lived first impressions are and how difficult they are to alter.

The car-buying experience is notorious for making people feel inadequate, demoralized and often left with the pains of buyer's remorse. There is a tendency towards forced politeness that can feel condescending. Combine all of this with high-pressure sales tactics and it is no wonder people feel insecure about knowing enough to make a smart decision. It's a highly effective sales process calculated to get the desired result – to ensure you walk out of the dealership buying a car. But, like so much of twenty-first-century life, the internet has changed the game. There is so much buying data available, and so many easy-buying platforms to access, that the methods used by car dealership salespeople have had to change radically.

Steven took a friend to see a car salesperson. She was a tiny thing and hardly the image of the person you'd expect to meet in a showroom. At one point during his buying excursion, he asked his friend what she thought of the salesperson and she said, 'Oh, she's so adorable and enthusiastic!'

Adorable? Who calls a car salesperson adorable?

Steven was, however, not surprised. After all, by this point he had bought or helped others buy six cars from her. He knew that she understood the new challenges facing car dealers and had developed her own highly effective brand. She quickly figured out that intimidation was never going to work for her and was not the right approach at this point anyway and so she cultivated a friendly, knowledgeable, non-threatening 'big sister' persona that is genuine to who she appears to be. Her acceptance of her strengths (and weaknesses) allowed her to honestly share that enthusiasm for the cars she sells and keep the obvious pressure to a minimum by adopting an 'I'm on your side' approach. She even embraced the theatrics of the sales process by taking delight in giving you the impression that the dealership was almost losing money on the deal (no one really believes this, but it plays well into the narrative she constructs). The result let her use her charm offensive to be infectious and fun, turning the whole buying process on its head, and offered an experience markedly different than what might be expected.

Effective personal branding is the proactive, deliberate approach to develop the meaning you want to have in the eyes of others. The alternative is an involuntary, often situational perception that will define your brand for you, quite possibly in ways you won't appreciate or like and may well negatively shape future communications. Situational branding rarely comes out in your favour so the answer to the question, 'Do I really need a personal brand?' is a resounding 'yes'. You need to cultivate your personal brand or others will. Snap judgements and perceptions, while frustrating, are a real outgrowth of the pace of life today. Not fair, but it happens hundreds of millions of times a day. Clearly, ignoring your brand is not an option.

In the business world your brand comes through every time you speak, every time you interact, every time you send an email. The manifestation of the brand may change by stakeholder – you may demonstrate it differently with customers or clients, colleagues or the chairman, but you cannot be a brand chameleon. If you are, you will soon be seen as inauthentic and, unfortunately, that may well become your brand much to your credibility capital detriment.

And, of course, your brand comes through in a prepared presentation and is more than getting the words right. Your command of the material, your presence, your perceived comfort level will all be demonstrations of your brand promise and differentiators. In smaller encounters, people are doing the same thing on a smaller level. What they know of your brand from the past, combined with what they experience in the present, either reinforces or contradicts your brand. Think of your brand as the shortcut to that meaning.

There are scores of articles and books on personal branding. Most focus on the development of leadership skills. Personal branding is, however, important no matter where you are in your career journey. At its heart, your personal brand is your credibility. Actions speak louder than words when it comes to your brand and they are remembered far longer.

Think about how you communicate your brand. It goes far beyond the ubiquitous elevator speech. Your brand is not a tagline. The promise of your brand will only take you so far. A powerful brand is based consistently on delivering that promise. Don't deliver on that brand and you will find your credibility capital balance will go to zero. Quite the ignominious end.

As in the case of the car salesperson, your brand is your reputation as expressed by others who have dealt with you. Remember, a brand isn't what the owner of that brand says it is, it's what others perceive it to be. So, think about how you react when in a group, how you take criticism, how you treat others because all of these actions are interpreted as being part of your brand.

We are never in complete control over how our brand is perceived. Outside factors have an impact, so you need to pay attention and regularly monitor your brand. This means checking your social media profile and knowing what others may be saying about you. When there is a political kerfuffle at your organization, understand how you came out at the end. Know whether you are being acknowledged or bad-mouthed. Pay attention to the tone and frequency of hall talk.

Brand perceptions are in constant flux. There is a tension, a good tension, between a long-standing brand and one that is cutting edge and responsive to change. Stay too long in that comfortable safe and dependable brand space and you run the risk of becoming irrelevant. Managing your brand effectively means being agile, adept and aware. And it requires doing regular brand audits.

Of course, you are always conducting a kind of mini-brand audit if you pay attention to how others react to you. That is a surface evaluation happening in real time. It gives you real-time information, but it is what researchers call a lagging indicator, rather than a leading indicator. A leading indicator is more valuable and impactful because it gives you a heads-up early on about the direction things are taking. A lagging indicator, however, tells you what has already happened. A frequently used example is a passenger yelling at a driver that the car is going much too fast and needs to slow down. The lagging indicator? Well, that would be the siren and lights of the police signalling the car to pull over and that a speeding ticket is in the future of the driver. Leading indicators tend to be small signals, easy to miss if you are not looking. Suddenly you are getting fewer invitations to lunch. Your email in basket isn't quite so full. People don't drop into your office as much as they once did. Your phone calls and texts are returned two or three days late or not at all.

Lagging indicators are bigger. You discover there have been weeks of important, high-profile meetings to which you were not invited. Projects you would usually lead are assigned to someone else. You find you are not asked to present to key clients or customers. The biggest lagging indicator of all? You did not receive the promotion you were certain was yours for the taking. In short, if you see a marked decline in the perception of your ability to inspire and motivate, manage and lead, it could be the result of a faltering brand.

> While at Hughes Aircraft Company, Rebecca once worked for a man named Joe Sanders, the EVP of the Space and Communications Group which was the satellite manufacturing business. She had recently finished as project manager the first communication survey of all 10,000 employees. The results were close to abysmal and justified the creation of a new position – manager of employee communication – but HR and the President of the Group did not know where to position the role within the business so they assigned Rebecca to him as his one and only direct report. That made Rebecca an organizational oddity for which Sanders had no real frame of reference.
>
> Over the next year, Rebecca worked on a variety of projects, including the largest open house ever held, almost 9,000 visitors. She began weekly lunches with the executives and employees. She created a schedule of walk-arounds for the leaders to meet with employees where they worked. She met with all of the division

managers individually to address the issues of their organizations raised in the communication survey. She created a new logo, launched a new magazine, revised the annual State of the Group presentation so it was more personal and more responsive to employee feedback – all in the course of 12 months.

Because she worked for him, Sanders had to do her performance reviews. At the first one he said, 'I gave you the highest rating and raise I could because there is one thing we know about you, Rebecca. We can give you any kind of project and you will exceed on the results and bring it in on time and on budget.'

Rebecca was flabbergasted. She knew she did excellent work, but it never occurred to her that this was the kind of personal brand she had developed. She took it to heart, however, and consciously worked to maintain the perception of her brand. Over the course of the next couple of years that brand earned her the promotion to another newly created position, that of corporate director of executive and employee communication working directly with the CEO.

Personal brands matter!

The first step in a brand audit is to determine just what your brand is and what you want it to be. You must let go of your ego, your pride and your reluctance to learn unpleasant truths. Here are the classic fundamentally challenging questions to consider when thinking about your personal brand. Consider these:

- What are my differentiators and what makes me influential? What is my role in my organization or specific situation? How do people see me? Where do I hold the most credibility? Do others see my differentiators as I see them?
- What traits do I have that people respect and acknowledge? Do I behave consistently with regard to those traits? Do my audiences and stakeholders value different traits? Do I understand what these are?
- How politically savvy am I? How perceptive am I in understanding other people's brands?

- Am I communicating effectively? Am I authentic? Do I share hard truths such that people accept them and feel supported? Am I perceived as being credible?
- What is my personal history? What are the significant experiences that have affected me? How have I acted and reacted in a variety of situations over time? Am I consistent? Do I demonstrate reliability?

As you think about these questions, note they are all about understanding your uniqueness and your differentiators. You have a brand, now take control of it.

Successful monitoring of your most personal of attributes is a tricky thing. You need the honesty of someone who will give you the unfiltered truth. This can be a useful leading indicator if you are ready to hear what might be hurtful or disappointing. It's important to remember, however, that a company's agenda with regard to how you fit into an organization may not always be in line with what you desire your brand to be. You may think your skills and talents suit you to particular positions. The company may be looking for something different. What that something different is, is what you need to understand and measure against your personal brand. Performance appraisals are a helpful indicator of how you are being perceived. Those evaluations might not be precisely focused on your brand, but they can be extremely helpful in giving you feedback you can use to modify how you are being perceived. Seek out and embrace the tools at your disposal. Human Resources may be able to provide personal assessment tools such as DiSC Personality Tests and 360 Assessment platforms which can be quite enlightening. Ask your boss for periodic feedback. All of these may not provide the complete picture of your personal brand, but they can be a vital component.

This is a book about communication, and you have to remember that a big part of communication is action, not words. And that is also true of the cultivation of your true brand. Actions are interpreted and have meaning for those who look to you for your opinion and guidance. Your words *and* your actions are what go into the making of your brand. It is a major part of your credibility and it helps you build trust. A strong, consistent personal brand is a powerful weapon in your communication and credibility arsenal.

BRANDING TIPS FOR YOUR COMMUNICATION STYLE

How You Prepare Information	
Meticulous	*Holistic*
What Likely Works for You	What Likely Works for You
Having a brand of meticulousness means people know you will have the details, the statistics, the evidence ready to support your point of view. Scrupulous in your preparation, you've thought through the presentation, the back-up and the back-up for the back-up and your audience knows it. It is a strong brand that brings credibility to the fore.	Yours is the visionary brand. A big picture thinker, you describe the ideas and possibilities available from them. Imaginative, inventive and instinctive, your reputation is about looking around the corner and describing what could be. The quintessential winger, you are confident in your ability to think on your feet and inspire people with your prescient possibilities.
What to Watch Out For	What to Watch Out For
A detail-oriented brand can be highly effective as a brand as long as it doesn't devolve into a perception of being picky, finicky or pedantic. Precision is all well and good, but don't lose the big-picture forest for the detailed trees. Help people see how your approach folds up into overall strategic objectives. This will add depth to your credibility and brand.	Inspiration and innovation are all well and good, but at some point, people want to know just what you will do. You might not want to bother with data and research, but you need to show that your vision and your brand are grounded in reality. Watch for over-confidence as that is a sure credibility killer. You do not have to give a step-by-step process but do give an overview and guidelines. It will add weight to your brand.
How You Convey Information	
Direct	*Diplomatic*
What Likely Works for You	What Likely Works for You
If direct communication is part of your brand, that will serve you well. You are likely perceived to be a straight talker, who neither prevaricates nor dissembles. This can build your reputation as an authentic speaker who is clear about what you believe and why you believe it.	A reputation for diplomacy can be a powerful add to your brand. You have a point of view, but you are aware that others have theirs as well. You don't want to present yours in a way that shuts others down. Because of this, people see you as open, willing to hear others' ideas and perspectives. People feel welcome to engage and they do.

What to Watch Out For	What to Watch Out For
Being direct can mean that you don't leave room for others to share their perspectives. You are prone to speak with such confident certainty that others are intimidated to engage. Don't stop being direct by any means, but do work on creating communication space for others to enter the arena. You just might find that being open to others' perspectives actually builds your brand and your credibility capital.	The opposite side of the diplomatic brand coin can be that you are indirect and obtuse in your communication. Wanting to be sure you do not offend can mean that you do not stand your rhetorical ground. Your language choices can be so subtle as to make your point of view easily overlooked. So, speak your mind – people can handle it.

How You Receive Communication

Relational	*Substantive*
What Likely Works for You	What Likely Works for You
You are attentive to what others are saying and this is likely a key element of your brand. You actually listen to people. You aren't thinking so much about what you will say when they are talking, but focusing on them. This is a positive brand differentiator and will build credibility capital.	Your brand is all about clarity. You listen for the essence of the conversation, presentation or question and answer session. You are able to identify misunderstandings and clarify. You are thoughtful in explaining away objections. Your brand is simple: content is king.
What to Watch Out For	What to Watch Out For
All well and good to listen carefully but be wary of letting it impede achieving your own goals. Too much focus on what you are hearing without using it to understand how it impacts, supports or refutes your position can result in not achieving your own objectives. People may like you and your brand, but that doesn't necessarily mean they will follow you if you aren't being clear on how and why they should.	Content may be king, but it should never be separated from those presenting it. By not paying attention to the person communicating, you may well miss vital cues that will help you understand what is behind the words. Add a little bit of active listening to your brand promise and you may well find you have increased your credibility capital.

How You Relate to Others	
Collaborative	*Independent*
What Likely Works for You	What Likely Works for You
Your brand is all about others. No doubt you are described as a people-person for your desire to engage. You look for ways to move towards consensus. You see compromise not as concession but as conciliation. Your brand, and your credibility capital, rest on your ability to bring people together.	Your brand logo might be a single drummer because that is what you march to. Not necessarily detached, you are pretty autonomous. People are apt to see your brand as consistent and self-reliant and quite focused on achieving your desired results. They know what to expect from you and that builds credibility capital.
What to Watch Out For	What to Watch Out For
Being the peacemaker can be quite satisfying but unless that is your job description, it can work against achieving your own ends. Be willing to broaden your brand just a touch by inserting yourself into the discussion as a participant and an advocate. It will add to your credibility capital.	Your drummer might have a little sign on his drum that says 'rigid', however. You can easily move from consistent to insistent if people do not seem to be falling in behind you. Your confidence in your own thought processes can blind you to others' perspectives, desires and wants. Take a breath and absorb what you are hearing. Let people know their ideas have merit. It will expand your brand and your credibility capital.

Your Communication Personality	
Animated	*Controlled*
What Likely Works for You	What Likely Works for You
The life and soul of the party, you are engaging, appealing and often disarming; people like to be around you. You tend to be persuasive and disarming. This makes you seem authentic and focused, which can be a very winning brand.	You value constraint. You are more sub-dued in your style and your approach to communication. Your brand is one of disciplined and focused communi-cation. People expect you to have all of your rhetorical ducks in a row and you usually do. That consistency helps build credibility capital.

What to Watch Out For	What to Watch Out For
All of these brand components can become disadvantages if you don't present yourself as serious and substantive when the situation calls. You can easily slip into seeming self-absorption if you don't pay attention to the essence of the discussion rather than the trappings. Learning versatility to master a more serious appearance when appropriate will build both your brand and your credibility capital.	You prioritize reaching your goals, but when unchecked, can alienate others. You may be perceived as reserved, or worse, indifferent to the perspectives of others. You may notice that people don't reach out to you to discuss issues and proposals, a sure sign they do not think you are open to others' views. Try reaching out yourself more often and solicit others' opinions. You may find that this not only adds to your brand and credibility capital, but also makes room for people to listen more openly to what you have to say.

7

Storytelling

Humans have a deep, instinctive affinity for narratives. Parents learn early that kids gravitate to stories, from *Goldilocks and the Three Bears* to *Little Red Riding Hood* to *The Very Hungry Caterpillar* to the adventure of Noah and scores of other religious tales. For a lot of us, those stories remain with us long after childhood is left behind. Stories are really just another way of communicating information, but they are far more engaging and powerful than facts or data alone. Stories entertain; they teach and reinforce the lessons we have learned. They shape our perception of the world.

So, why is this penchant for storytelling so strong and why does it play such a powerful role in how we communicate and think? For centuries, researchers and thinkers have puzzled over these questions and we now have important insight into the answers. Research in neuroscience suggests that it starts at a biological level: engaging stories activate our attention and emotion in unique ways that make us more likely to be moved to action. Incorporating health information into entertainment has become an effective tool in driving behaviour change.[1] Communication scholars such as Walt Fisher suggest that human communication has always been fundamentally about stories. In his theory of the Narrative Paradigm, Fisher suggests that stories are 'symbolic interpretations of aspects of the world occurring in time and shaped by history, culture, and character'.[2] In short, we use stories to make sense of our world.

Over the years, the concept of storytelling has made its way into everyday business life and branding. In fact, a quick internet search for books on storytelling finds books on the topic in such diverse areas as marketing, science, technology, children, presentations and business in general. This is not that surprising given that as the research makes clear, stories are often the best way to make a lasting impression, so it's not surprising that most successful and recognizable brands are those that tell a story.[3] What is surprising is how little thought we tend to give stories as part of our own individual communication strategies. Especially in a professional setting, it can be easy to get so wrapped up in the facts that we lose sight of how we are engaging our audience.

[1]Sood, Suruchi, Henderson Riley, Amy & Alarcon, Kristine Cecile (2017), 'Entertainment-Education and Health and Risk Messaging', in *Oxford Research Encyclopedia of Communication*, Oxford University Press, https://doi.org/10.1093/acrefore/9780190228613.013.245

[2]Fisher, Walter R. (1984), 'Narration as a Human Communication Paradigm: The Case of Public Moral Argument', *Communication Monographs* 51, No. 1: 1–22, https://doi.org/10.1080/03637758409390180

[3]Nakhil, Rania Farouk Abdel Azim. International Journal of Innovation and Applied Studies; Rabat Vol. 26, Iss. 4, (Jul 2019): 1346-1357.

Facts are critical, but in a sense, they are just the play-by-play and without the colour commentary. It is in our choice and delivery of stories that we communicate most effectively and personally.

We tend to instinctively choose a story to make a point. When asked about our day, for example, we tell a story. Not that we think of it as a story, it's just what happened. Like most of life, however, it isn't really that simple. Stories are always coloured by our memories and perceptions. Ask adult siblings about a shared childhood holiday memory and it quickly becomes apparent they might as well have been on different trips. Their recollections and descriptions are based on what was important to them in the experience. This is why stories are so personal – perspectives emerge from every recollection and those perspectives speak volumes about us.

So, how do you take advantage of stories to make an impact? You do that by approaching the choice strategically. With the right preparation, weaving a story into a speech, presentation or interview can increase your power, influence and credibility. Perhaps the best examples are found in the world of talk shows. Think for a moment about the best guests on a talk show, like Jennifer Lawrence or Will Smith or Ricky Gervais. These are supremely talented actors and performers, but their real secret weapon as a talk show guest is found in their arsenal of stories. Stories give them a natural and entertaining platform to showcase their personalities, build a relationship with their audience and, of course, promote whatever it is they're there to plug. In fact, stories are so vital to a successful appearance that there are actually producers whose job it is to select and prep them in advance. (Now that you know this, you'll never watch a talk show in the same way again – you'll just be waiting for those stories.)

Chances are you don't have the luxury of a producer guiding your every step, but you can be just as strategic in selecting the stories to tell to get you the results you're after. While you may never be on a national talk show, the principles for finding and using good stories are the same. Obviously, stories will vary in topic, tone and length, but all effective storytelling does three key things: it helps the audience *identify* with you, it builds and keeps their *attention* and it makes them *feel* something. Those pillars hold up in all kinds of contexts. Keep that basic formula in mind when you make any kind of appearance, whether in a hall in front of 1,000 people, a business presentation or just networking at a cocktail party, and you'll be able to find a story that will help you command credible attention in support of the points you want to make.

First, stories should be personal and relatable. Include experiences such as overcoming a challenge, how you took your first step in your chosen profession or something that references the journey of a family member (hopefully, with their permission, of course) will help the audience identify with you. Second, the story must conclude with something related to your goal. And last, your story must connect your audience to the specific takeaways you've predetermined for the presentation. Never forget you are using the story to first and foremost illustrate a point, so the reason for telling the story must return the audience to your overall mission. If it's a remarkable story but doesn't reinforce your message, it risks becoming just an entertaining waste of time.

Stories or narratives are not the content of your presentation or talk, rather they are key signposts on the journey you are taking audiences on towards your ultimate point. Make sure that the reward at the end justifies the length of the journey. Identifying these story signposts can be tricky if you are just beginning to take strategic advantage of narrative, so test your stories on someone you trust. Make sure your story is clear, concise and cogent. Tangents are message killers, the quickest way to lose an audience. Even great speakers can get off-track easily, especially when they have told the same stories over and over again. You want to get in and get out of the story, so you don't dilute its impact on your presentation and your audience's minds.

Clearly defining what you need to accomplish and how to use stories that support it will help you avoid the pitfalls of tangents and strengthen the core of your credibility. As you develop your strategy, you can take a page from literary archetypes to figure out what kind of story best suits your goals. Admittedly it's a deep dive into the storytelling process, but these frameworks are extremely useful templates.

ARCHETYPES

It's long been known that character development in literature is based on archetypal figures with traits that make those characters consistent, believable – and yes, credible. Webster defines archetype as 'the original pattern or model of which all things of the same type are representations or copies ... also: a perfect example'.[4] When we see these archetypes, we have a natural recognition of the patterns they represent. We find archetypes throughout history, but it wasn't until the early twentieth century that the Swiss renowned psychiatrist and psychologist Carl Jung took a more structured approach to the accepted practice of analysing characters and their behaviour in literature by creating 12 archetypal categories. What brought Jung's nomenclature such widespread notoriety was that the groupings seemed universal and worked as a kind of shortcut to meaning.[5] Stories that are based in the archetypes work because they are intuitively understood by the audience and allow your story to make an instant connection with them. They make a connection to the mind in a way that facts and figures do not. In your own communication, it isn't so much that you need to 'play' or take on an archetypal role as it is about thinking about which narrative archetype best serves your context and goals. So, as you're preparing, consider which of Jung's archetypes provides the most impactful framework to communicate your message. Remember, archetypes are shortcuts to audience engagement. Once you identify the archetype, you can move on to the story selection process:

Caregiver – A comforting message featuring a 'parent-like' character who desires to protect the group. These stories demonstrate the ability to provide security.

Creator – An inspiring, creative message that relies on innovation and vision to command the crowd. These are stories of originality and insight that capture people's imagination.

Explorer – An experimental, adventurous perspective from someone who needs to be on the edge and is uncomfortable with conforming. These stories of exciting exploration take people on a journey to the unknown.

[4]https://www.merriam-webster.com/dictionary/archetype
[5]Jung, C.G. (author), Hull, R.F.C. (translator), (1981), *The Archetypes and The Collective Unconscious* (Collected Works of C.G. Jung Vol.9 Part 1) Collected Works of C.G. Jung (48).

Hero – A hero proves his worth by personally rescuing others, but also flourishes as part of a unit. Hero stories are those of champions and teams who beat the odds in achieving success.

Innocent – Stories that feature eternal optimists who always seek to do the right thing despite a world of negativity. These are the tales that take us into the visionary world of the possible.

Jester – Stories from the perspective of those who are pretty much dedicated to having a good time and always look to bring that same degree of delight and levity to others. Droll, funny, often absurd, these stories lighten the mood and can relieve tension between opposing points of view.

Lover – Lovers tend to want to please others at any cost. They are fiercely loyal and generally looking to winning others' affections. These stories demonstrate devotion, reliability and dedication and the points made focus outwards.

Magician – This character is a visionary like *The Creator* but operates within the system and understands the politics necessary for success. They can convey the messaging of charismatic leadership or effective persuasion. These are stories of magnetism and charm that also subtly address the political demands of the situation.

Orphan – As the name suggests, these stories centre mostly on the fears of being left out of decisions and not being rewarded for what someone has to offer. *Orphans* try so hard to fit in that they often lose their own identities. These stories are often grounded in empathy but need to be carefully crafted such that there is resonance and authenticity.

Rebel – The messaging of disrupters, the revolutionaries who believe that the only way to achieve success is to turn things on their heads. Rebels move fast and break things. Groundbreaking, unconventional and unexpected, these stories challenge the audience's sense of the world.

Ruler – Stories that resonate from the perspective of those who want and need to decide almost everything themselves and for everyone else. While this may come from a confidence born of a sense of knowing better and being smarter, when all is said and done, these are stories of domination. They demonstrate past personal and business successes based on individualistic decisions made, actions taken and results achieved.

Sage – The intellectual approach to most issues. Sage stories are thoughtful and self-reflective and are critical of ignorance more than anything else. Introspective, reflective and contemplative, these analytical stories are grounded in data and information.

This is not just an abstract exercise, using these archetypal frameworks for stories has proved beneficial for scores of our clients.

The founder of a new software company was giving a presentation to his board of directors. He needed to be telling 'Creator' stories that supported him as the right visionary to discover new talent and change the way people searched for video content. He needed to demonstrate that he was a technologist who was adept at cultivating relationships with filmmakers. Steven encouraged him to tell stories about his time in film school, apparently being one of the first students in his class to edit his projects on a laptop, and how he started and managed film festivals, which gave a platform for new directors. These stories enabled his BoD to buy into his vision and his capabilities.

A retired FBI counter-terrorism agent about to start a new career as a pundit came to Steven to help him find stories for his anticipated speeches and TV appearances. Steven started, as always, by assessing who the audience was and what the goal was. It made sense that those who would watch him on a show or would pay to hear him speak wanted to hear stories about overcoming danger and saving others: he needed 'Hero' stories. We pressed him to tell a story about how he felt when he first arrived at Quantico, the FBI academy. He said he was completely intimidated by the legendary G-Men (agents) that founded the organization and unsure whether he had enough personal conviction to put his life on the line if ever asked to do so. But, in the end, his years of training, which came immediately after the first World Trade Center bombing in 1993, brought out his dedication. Ultimately, he was assigned to work in the White House with the group that ran terrorist scenarios for the West Wing, where he had a distinguished career. Once he connected with these stories, he realized he did have the material he needed right there in his head.

A much different example is found in our work with Leslie Iwerks, an established documentary filmmaker who is the granddaughter of Walt Disney's first business partner and co-creator/animator of Mickey Mouse. When she was invited to give a TEDx Talk in Torino, Italy, about her filmmaking career and family background, she felt it was important to share her connection with her grandfather's story thoughtfully and authentically. Steven concluded she needed to tell stories from the perspective of a 'Caregiver' to demonstrate her big-picture protection of his legacy. She was sharing undocumented history: stories of how Walt and her grandfather formed an animation business together as teenagers that led to multiple cartoon series in Hollywood and then to the infamous design that became Disney's most famous cartoon character. Her stories were peppered with charmingly sentimental and personal details. She reminisced about being a kid and having the Disney Studios backlot and the Disneyland Park as her personal week-end playgrounds, and described her delight when her father (a designer and engineer at the Disney Studio) brought home life-like rubber moulds of his hands that were to be the actual hands of the audio-animatronic Abraham Lincoln figure from Disneyland's attraction 'Great Moments with Mr. Lincoln'. As a kid, she found great joy in hiding the hands for fun – in desk drawers, under chairs or in the refrigerator – for her friends, parents and teachers to discover, much to their dismay! All of these fun stories allowed her to share a very personal side of growing up behind the scenes at 'Disney' and she even named her TEDx Talk 'Stories Meant to be Told'.

Each of these individuals was able to clarify and strengthen their strategic message by thoughtfully choosing the archetypes that supported the aspects of themselves and their messages that they wanted to highlight.

Think about the archetypes as you are putting together your outline and deciding on a story that will engage and capture your audience's attention. Don't focus too narrowly on the label, think of the archetype descriptions above as broad templates for your story selections. Which one best helps bring your audience along with you to the happy ending you're aiming for?

These archetypes will give you an important leg-up in designing the stories that works best for your communication context and goals, but two reminders are in order as you set off:

First, remember that personal is powerful. People react and are more engaged and open to persuasion if they feel a connection to a character – or, in this case, you as the speaker.[6] But there is such a thing as too personal. You want to avoid TMI – Too Much Information. A good story sets boundaries so you seem open but does not reveal so much that your audience starts to feel either awkward or manipulated. Your story should engender an emotional connection without making the listener uncomfortable.

Second, remember what we said about all the prep work that goes into those seemingly spontaneous anecdotes on talk shows? Confidence that your stories will deliver strong, lasting impact is really only achieved with preparation and practice. The best storytellers have told their definitive stories countless times and gained a sense of people's reaction and they are clear in their own minds as to what they want that story to achieve. A good, well-practised storyteller is rewarded with a special brand of credibility and can have significant influence so, make sure you use your stories frequently – that will help your ease of delivery.

Telling a story is one of the most powerful ways to establish your credibility, reach your audience and get your message across. And

---

[6]Berger, Charles R., Michael E. Roloff, and David R. Ewoldsen, eds. *The handbook of communication science.* Sage, 2010.

remember, it is *your* story. We all get to be the producers, screenwriters and stars of our own autobiographical movies. In telling your story, you step away from your notes, your slides, your text and those are the moments of greatest credibility and power. Nothing is more effective in framing your message than stories which illustrate who you are and the lasting points you want to make.

STORYTELLING TIPS FOR YOUR COMMUNICATION STYLE

How You Prepare Information	
Meticulous	*Holistic*
What Likely Works for You	What Likely Works for You
Planner that you are, you build your communication thoughtfully from start to finish. This allows you to think about how narrative can be used to support your arguments. You might want to pay close attention to the archetypes. These may help you expand your story catalogue.	Big picture thinker that you are, you are drawn to narrative like the proverbial duck to water. Basically, you think in the narrative. This is your natural state as you are comfortable thinking on your feet and stories are often a natural outgrowth of that. This allows you to seemingly pull tales out of your hat as something occurs to you or the way the audience responds triggers the perfect story.
What to Watch Out For	What to Watch Out For
You are such a perfectionist, you may find yourself reviewing and revising and re-examining each story you think about using. Once you decide on them, however, you may find yourself unable to stop editing or rewriting. The solution here is to go against your grain and not write them out at all. Give yourself an outline or a note and trust that when it comes to telling the story, you've got this. It will make the story more interesting and increase your credibility capital because you have added just a little bit of spontaneity to your plan.	While your comfort level empowers your confidence that when you need a story it will appear, a little forethought will stand you in good stead. Think about the archetypes and how those concepts can make your stories more powerful. Remember to link both archetypes and stories to your ultimate communication objective. This will add to your credibility capital.

How You Convey Information

Direct

What Likely Works for You

You may not be the storyteller with the most flourishes, but when you think one is on point and focused, you will incorporate it. You view stories as examples to be used as evidence, adding to your straightforward approach to communication.

What to Watch Out For

You want to remind yourself that straightforward data, evidence and statistics are good for sharing in formation but less so in winning the proverbial hearts and minds. People need their imaginations engaged and stories are the way to do that. Think about the archetypes as ways to make arguments and you may find yourself more comfortable with adding storytelling to your repertoire.

Diplomatic

What Likely Works for You

You are a natural storyteller. After all, your communication pathway meanders a bit and what better way to meander than take the scenic route. You can use the concept of archetypes very effectively to ensure your stories hit their mark rather than just letting them flow.

What to Watch Out For

You pay attention to how others are reacting to you and this allows you to gauge their feedback. The challenge is not to let them distract you. If you expected a chuckle or a smile or an empathetic sigh from a story and did not get it, you may try to force it. Explaining something beyond its telling is a losing strategy. Evaluate why a story might not have resonated with the audience in your personal debrief afterwards – don't try to fix it in real time.

How You Receive Communication

Relational

What Likely Works for You

Stories bring people into your presentation. As you are one of those people who pays close attention to others, you will naturally take notice of how and when your audience reacts. This can help you gauge whether to go into more detail or cut your losses and move on. A story needs to resonate and the only way to be able to determine if it has is being in tune with your listeners. You do that by listening to them, even if what you are listening to is non-verbal.

Substantive

What Likely Works for You

Your attention is on your material and you know exactly what it is you are determined to achieve. Your audience knows this and expects this from you. So, start to think about how stories can be woven into that formula. You want to engender more overt response from the audience, so you know whether or not they are buying what you are selling.

What to Watch Out For	What to Watch Out For
You pay attention to the audience and that is all well and good – until it takes you on to the tangential highway. You may find the audience is so receptive that you start sharing more. Stories are the icing on the rhetorical cake, too many of those empty calories takes away from the essence of the talk. Use them as support, don't let them become a diversion from your real mission.	Your talks are focused on the data, the logic and the evidence that forms the basis of your arguments. Stories are not your natural stock in trade, but if you think about the archetypes and your goals, you can find the perfect anecdotes to add some pizzazz. You may find that when you do, your audience sits up a little straighter, leans a little closer as your stories become the entry way to your well-reasoned thoughts.

How You Relate to Others

Collaborative	*Independent*
What Likely Works for You	What Likely Works for You
You are apt to look for stories that demonstrate how others have addressed topics you are discussing. Given your general empathetic approach, you try to engender that same reaction in your listeners. You look for analogous narratives that can allow your audience to see themselves in the stories. You can use archetypes effectively if you apply them correctly to how your audience can be emotionally moved. This will add depth and richness to your credibility capital.	When and if you decide to use stories, you will make sure they fit your content overall. Given that your focus is reaching your goals and objectives, your material – data and information – is chosen carefully to build to your obvious conclusion. Use this same focus to add stories to the mix. Think about the archetypes to trigger stories that will add emotional depth to your talk.
What to Watch Out For	What to Watch Out For
You may need to remind yourself that analogies are tricky things. Not everyone, maybe even not a majority, of your listeners will see themselves or their situation in your story. Given your collaborative nature, you may easily assume that others will see the same similarities in your stories that you do. A dangerous assumptive road to take. Pay close attention to your audience and their backgrounds. The more you know about them, the more likely you are to hit the analogy nail on the head.	The notion of stories may be a bit alien to you because your approach is logic over emotion. Remember, while stories can engage the audience's emotions, they can also bring more abstract concepts to life. You may be well served to think about the archetypes in terms of how you want your listeners to perceive you as well as how they can engage audience attention. Remember, their perceptions and your credibility capital are inextricably linked.

Your Communication Personality	
Animated	*Controlled*
What Likely Works for You	What Likely Works for You
You very often are the story. Even when you are not engaging in narrative per se, your very style adds verve to a talk. When you use stories, they are often personal experiences or examples. You may want to expand to stories in which you are not the rhetorical star. Look for stories outside of your experience and give them your same dynamic treatment. This puts you and your audience in the same perspective of the story. It helps make you one of them – a very persuasive perspective.	You just naturally keep emotion in check. In fact, your more animated colleagues probably make you crazy. You can use stories in a focused, controlled manner that add to your credibility but don't move you into that uncomfortable range. Think about the archetypes as another source for content. Pick them using two criteria: 1. How do you want the audience to perceive you? What persona actually makes your presentation of your content more credible? 2. What kinds of archetypal stories will resonate with your audience such that they are more prone to follow you all the way to your conclusion? You already do this with your content, just add this layer to make yourself even more effective.
What to Watch Out For	What to Watch Out For
Dynamic style that you have, you may have the tendency to move talk into the realm of performance. Humorous stories are likely one of your stocks in trade and when the audience eats it up, you may be triggered to move from presenter to stand-up comic. But don't! Keep the stories on point, humorous or not, and remember, your aim is not applause but achieving your goal.	Your biggest barrier to stories may be your own belief that stories are nowhere near as persuasive as data. Be careful of using yourself as a focus group of one. The data are pretty clear, people reason through stories. So, you like data, right? Take this piece to your rhetorical heart and watch the increase in your credibility capital!

8

Non-Verbal Communication

Whether discussed as body language or kinesics or non-verbal communication, most people understand that there is more to communication than the words they use. Researchers have spent decades attempting to quantify the impact of non-verbal communication – with mixed results.

In 1967, Mehrabian and Ferris suggested a formula for this quantification. They posited that verbal was a mere 7 per cent of meaning created in communication, while vocal impact was 38 per cent and facial a whopping 55 per cent.[1] While referenced in myriad textbooks and studies, the exactness of this formula has led to other researchers questioning its methodology and specificity.[2] There is no disagreement among researchers or practitioners of communication, however, that non-verbal messaging has a significant role to play in the creation of meaning. Your non-verbal communication is going to affect your credibility capital and as such, needs to be understood within the context of your workplace communication culture and, to the extent you can, managed.

Non-verbal communication ranges from vocal tone to clothing to gestures to time. Depending on the circumstance, not all elements will have equal impact on your credibility. Over time, however, all will have an impact on how you are perceived and how successful you are in influencing others. So, it is important that you understand what the elements of non-verbal communication are, how these are interpreted and what you can do to manage them so you can ensure you are banking, credibility capital.

There are seven elements of non-verbal communication we will discuss here:

- Chronemics – time;
- Haptics – touch;
- Kinesics – movement;
- Objectics – clothing, artifacts and objects;
- Oculesics – eye contact;
- Proxemics – physical space;
- Vocalics – voice, separate from words.

---

[1]Mehrabian, Albert (1 January 1968), 'Some Referents and Measures of Nonverbal Behaviour', *Behaviour Research Methods & Instrumentation* 1, No. 6: 203–7, https://doi.org/10.3758/BF03208096

[2]Burgoon, Judee K., Buller, David B. & Woodall, William Gill (1 January 1997), *Nonverbal Communication: The Unspoken Dialogue*, 2nd ed, New York: McGraw-Hill, 1996; Lapakko, David, 'Three Cheers for Language: A Closer Examination of a Widely Cited Study of Nonverbal Communication', *Communication Education* 46, No. 1: 63–67, https://doi.org/10.1080/03634529709379073

CHRONEMICS

Whenever you have travelled outside of your own country you have no doubt experienced how diverse cultures approach time differently. Some have a rigid view of time – if the train leaves at 8:12, it leaves at 8:12. Others have a more lenient and flexible relationship to time with 'on time' being within 20 minutes of what is planned. While we are not going to discuss general cultural norms here, we are going to look at how organizations' approach to time varies and how you can ensure you stay within the lines of what is accepted and expected.

Time rigidity is likely the most noticeable element workplace chronemics. As discussed, knowing whether meetings begin on time or a few minutes after affects your reputation and credibility. A general rule of thumb is that you do not lose by arriving a few minutes early, whether the expectation of time is rigid or flexible. Time rigidity also affects the length of time of meetings. Do they end on time or go over? In the world of video meetings, time rigidity has overtaken flexibility. Spending a lot of time staring at the screen in Zoom or Microsoft Teams meetings has lessened people's tolerance for overtime discussion. In some systems, there are time limits for meetings, ending a meeting on time whether discussion is complete or not.

The last element of time rigidity or flexibility in organizations is found in presentation time limits. In a rigid perspective, your ten minutes are up at ten minutes. You may not get the proverbial hook, but you will certainly see some interesting non-verbal cues from participants as they fidget, start to look at their phones or otherwise stop paying attention.

Chronemics includes agenda setting. In a flexible time culture, meetings may have a topic but no agenda. Discussions may go off on tangents, fail to get to decision making or wander into uncharted waters. In organizations that are primarily creative and innovative, agendas may be perceived as stultifying and controlling. These cultures have a very flexible and adaptive relationship with time that they likely think is their competitive advantage. Rigid time cultures view time as a scarce resource to be managed and allocated consciously. Time is viewed as valuable and no more to be wasted than money. Agendas are a requirement in order to guarantee that time is never squandered. Meetings may not be short, but they are focused and the discussion is to the point. With regard to presentations, audiences generally have a poor sense of time. They just react to whether something feels too long or too short, which can often vary greatly from how much time has actually passed.

HAPTICS

COVID-19 changed the way people of all walks of personal and professional life thought about touching. From handshakes to friendly hugs, these signs of respect and affection became verboten as concerns about the virus spread. In fact, some public health experts suggest that getting rid of handshakes, unsanitary even in normal times, would go a long way towards eliminating the spread of the common cold and the annual flu virus.

All that said, touch will likely never be eliminated completely as an element of non-verbal communication. We won't discuss the issues around inappropriate touching except to say that it should never be tolerated. A pat on the back, an appropriate hug, a fist bump or touching elbows will likely remain as acceptable demonstrations of non-verbal haptics within a communication culture.

As in all non-verbal elements, there are cultural expectations surrounding touch. In more formal organizational cultures haptics is likely reduced to a handshake or, in some countries, a bow. Fist bumps carry a different kind of message and will tend to be found in more informal and casual organizations.

Touch, when appropriate and welcome, is an essential element of human connection. In the workplace, this connection has had layers over time of what constitutes appropriate and welcome. Eliminating all haptics eliminates an important relationship building block and likely will not vanish completely from organizational life. Violating haptic norms, however, is perhaps the most damaging non-verbal error one can make. Watch and learn and follow are the best courses of action you can take to ensure you do not stray from the acceptable cultural path.

KINESICS

Kinesics covers all manner of body movement. Loosely described in pop culture as 'body language', there is no doubt that gestures, stance and facial expressions stimulate meaning in the minds of others. Kinesics is important because while some of it is conscious, so much of it is unintentional. The interpretation in the mind of the receiver is often unconscious as well. That is the nature of first impressions, by the way. We take in all manner of stimuli when we meet someone for the first time, most of it in the non-verbal arena and much of it kinesics. So, understanding how it works, what it means and why it matters is going to be a linchpin to your credibility.

An important part of body movement are gestures. Whether giving a presentation, sitting around a conference table or staring into a computer screen, human beings move. Much of that comes in the form of hand and arm gesture, and they happen naturally and spontaneously. They are particularly important when speaking in public.

Illustrative gestures are those that work as a kind of visual aid. They add to the meaning of words by providing an extra bit of information. The fish was *this* big. There are *three* points I want to make. The *whole* group was excited. Can't you just see in your mind's eye what the gestures would be that would add to the meaning of the statements? It can be tempting to plan out the gestures but that would be the wrong inclination. Body movement should come of its own accord. Be mindful of advice such as 'you should use your hands more'. If it is unnatural for you, take it to heart, but be true to your own feelings. Those who get that direction have a tendency to overdo the suggestion and that can be distracting.

Gestures in public speaking can connote either nervousness or confidence, regardless of what you are feeling. Stand straight. Let your arms hang free so you can let the gestures come of their own accord. Above all, refrain from putting your hands in your pockets, on your hips or clasping them behind your back because if you do, you restrict your gestures. Keep your hands available so your thoughts and your words can trigger your gestures.

Facial expressions are a key visual aid in that when we speak with people in almost any setting their gaze is fixed on our face. Smiling can indicate warmth and good humour. Inappropriate smiling, at odds with the words spoken, calls into question intent and authenticity. A frown or stern expression may suggest a serious and perhaps unwelcome news conversation is in the works. Facial expressions can indicate thoughtfulness or grimness, lightheartedness or sombreness, humour or even intensity. The interpretations – yours or theirs – may be accurate, then again, they may not. So, don't worry about planning and practising your expressions. In general, you are best served if you relax your face and let your non-conscious mind take over the reins of facial expression.

Much body movement, including facial expressions, gestures, stance and posture, happens without our controlling it. This means that if there is a conflict between what we say and what our bodies do, the latter is often interpreted as revealing more of 'the truth'. Someone may smile at you and give you a handshake to congratulate you on your promotion, but you get the sense they do not mean it. You may not be able to describe why but you just know something is off. If you had a video playback, you might notice that the smile did not make it up to their eyes and the handshake was somewhat perfunctory and weak as they pulled away just a bit too quickly.

There are no hard and fast interpretive rules to body movement – pop psychology notwithstanding – but chances are good that what you feel in your gut may well be right. We reach conclusions based on feelings, but those feelings do not come from thin air. We absorb what others' bodies are doing and we make connections and determinations. They do the same to us. Be mindful, but know that you, and they, do not have complete control over all that makes up kinesics non-verbal communication.

OBJECTICS

Much as it sounds, objectics relates to the things of non-verbal communication. Objects, clothing, jewellery, headgear all are part of what others interpret beyond the words we say. Ironically, while this is the non-verbal element we have the most control over, it is often the one to which we pay the least attention. And like so many of the other elements, we may not take into account how these things in our life communicate non-verbally to others.

Whether it's 'dress for success' or 'the clothes maketh the man (or woman)', there is a more or less shared assumption that what we wear communicates. We just need to remember that what it meant to us when we put on the day's outfit may not mean the same thing to those we meet during the day – in person or on video conference.

In the workplace there are usually accepted dress codes: stated or understated. Certain cultures are traditionally formal and men wear suits and ties and women dresses or pantsuits. Sometimes there are subcultures, where some dress formally – the so-called 'suits' – and some dress less formally in jeans and T-shirts, working in manufacturing or research and development. You may never see anything written down describing what is and is not acceptable, but your credibility depends on you figuring it out. In general, if you are not sure, opt to go more formal. You can always take off a tie or jacket if it turns out a little more informality is appropriate.

Our office or cubicle spaces also speak volumes, so think about what you decorate and how. Consider the artwork and knick-knacks you display. As all of these items will be interpreted, you want to keep things sleek and focused. Photographs are fine, but leave out the beach party and put up a simple family shot. One or two diplomas or certificates are okay, too many starts to look like a wall of self-promotion. If yours is an office in which you meet with other people, think about what a messy desk communicates. You might think it shows that you are busy, productive and important. To others, it may show you are sloppy, disorganized, even unfocused. The truth might be in the middle, but that subtlety is likely to be lost on your visitors.

OCULESICS

Oculesics relates to the non-verbal communication produced by our eyes. Given that our eyes have been described as the windows to our souls, this is an essential facet to address. Eye contact, movement and gaze are the primary elements involved with oculesics.

Eye contact, or the lack thereof, is interpreted in myriad ways – and some of them even correctly. Some theorize that looking to the right means someone is lying, others that looking to the left shows fabrication. Still more suggest that looking up and away indicates untruthfulness. In all likelihood all of these are true for someone at some time but as a universal truth, it is useless to make assumptions based on any of these indicators. What is important to remember is that accurate or not, people will interpret your eye contact as indicating something important.

The best rule of thumb for eye contact is to maintain a steady but not staring gaze. Whether talking one-to-one or giving a presentation, looking at the people listening to you demonstrates an interest in them and a desire for connection. Furthermore, eye contact allows you to assess your listeners and determine if they are engaged with you.

Be careful of eye movement – rapidly shifting from right to left and back again is what gave rise to the phrase 'shifty-eyed'. It connotes untrustworthiness at best, untruthfulness at worst. Should you ever find yourself at a teleprompter, move your head and not your eyes as you go from the screen on the left to the screen on the right. It will make you look much more engaged and present. You may find yourself looking away, perhaps up, when answering a question or thinking of a point to be made. That can happen as we try to think uninterrupted by the upturned faces of our audience. It is a natural response but try to be sensitive to the impact it can have on those listening to you. Keep it short, resume eye contact and no harm done. Begin to answer to the ceiling tiles and you can likely feel your credibility capital account being drained.

Your eyes may or may not be the window to your soul, but they are definitely the straightest line between you and your audience. Make the most of that opportunity to connect and build your credibility.

PROXEMICS

Proxemics is the use of space and distance in communication. Where you choose to sit, how close or far you choose to stand from others are all part of this facet of non-verbal communication.

How close you stand to someone depends on the nature and intimacy of the relationship. We stand closest to family, furthest to strangers. When we cannot observe the rules of space comfort, such as in a crowded lift or jammed subway, we strive to create the illusion of space by looking away or straight ahead. This intersection of eye contact and space works together to soften the discomfort of prolonged eye contact with someone standing or sitting uncomfortably close.

When giving a presentation, we try not to stand too close to the people in front. Many conference rooms make this difficult as the space from the first row or table to the screen is often quite tight. Standing such that we are in line of the projector light, throwing our shadow onto the screen is equally problematic. Thus, checking out the meeting space prior to speaking is a good standard protocol. If you cannot do both – avoid the projector light and stand back from the closest people – apologize to the people in front and stand there. It is not ideal, but it is better than becoming part of your slides.

Where we sit is part of proxemics. Teachers and professors pay close attention to where students choose to sit themselves. Rightly or wrongly, there is an assumption often made that those who go as far to the back of the room as possible are looking to escape detection and be as unnoticed as possible. Those up front? They get the more positive assumption of being engaged and interested and bright. Assumptions all, but they may drive the faculty member's perceptions of the students in the class throughout the semester.

In the workplace, where one sits becomes most noticeable around the conference table. Often the leader sits at the head of the table, the senior people sit at the table and the more junior or less important participants sit in the chairs around the wall. When appropriate, you may request a position of control at the head of the table if you need the commanding attention of the room for a presentation. While there may be cultural exceptions to these standards in some organizations, you are likely to find that these are few and far between. Pay attention in new situations, however – you never know when the expectations will be upended.

VOCALICS

It may seem strange to discuss the voice as part of non-verbal communication, but 'paralanguage', as it is often called, refers not to *which* words are spoken but *how* they are spoken. After all, the way you say a word can vastly change the meaning. You can say, 'It's fine' and it can mean all is good, all is questionable but will work out, or all is totally ruined, depending on your tone of voice. To understand how our voice communicates beyond our words, we need to look at pitch, volume, rate, pauses and quality. Tone could be thought of as the 'emoji' of verbal messaging.

Pitch refers to how high or low our voice is. In general, we do not pay close attention to our own pitch – except when we hear a playback of ourselves. We do not sound anywhere near as good as when we hear ourselves. This is because we hear ourselves through the best sound system ever devised, our skulls. Listening to yourself can make you unnecessarily self-conscious about something you can do little about, therefore we don't advise it. Most men have a lower natural pitch, most women higher. Former British Prime Minister Margaret Thatcher altered the pitch and tone of her voice very effectively. While, like Thatcher, you can learn to adjust the pitch of your voice for dramatic value, if it does not come across as natural it is fraught with credibility peril. Therefore, sticking with the pitch your vocal cords naturally give you is quite likely your best way forward. A rise in pitch, particularly in the beginning or middle of a sentence can be an uncontrollable side effect of nervousness. Beware of that 'tell' and understand the more familiar you are with the material, the more natural you will sound. A rise in pitch at the end of a sentence can often suggest a question or uncertainty while a steady pitch is generally more authoritative and credible.

We tend not to notice volume until we hear someone in broadcast mode speaking much more loudly than is normal or desirable. In general, we do not ask them to speak more quietly although we will ask someone who is speaking too quietly to speak up. This is ironic as listening to someone practically shouting at us is extremely uncomfortable. We may have to struggle to pick up the words from someone speaking softly, but it is not likely to make our head ache. Watch the people near you – they will give you their own non-verbal signals if you are speaking in too ear-splitting a manner.

The rate of our speaking has an impact on our listeners. If we speak too slowly, they may find their attention wandering. In some situations, you might find someone prompting you speed up by finishing off your thought. This helpfulness is rarely welcomed or appreciated, so avoid inadvertently making the same mistake to another. Speaking too fast makes us sound frenetic, frenzied and unsure of ourselves. While the human brain can think faster than anyone can talk, it can be exhausting to listen to. Keep your rate even: neither feverishly fast nor painfully slow.

The last element of vocalics lies in the quality of our voice. Affected by how the air comes over our vocal folds, a voice can be breathy or hoarse, melodious or rough, thin or chesty. Intricately connected to pitch, but not the same, this is the element most difficult to change without professional assistance. Speech pathologists are the experts who can work with those whose vocal quality is problematic and hurts their credibility. While we may not love the quality of our own voice, in truth most of us have perfectly acceptable vocal quality, so relax.

Non-verbal communication is going to be a major contributor or detractor to your credibility, both in what you do that others interpret and what others do that you interpret. The rules are more diverse than consistent. Paying attention and understanding the norms around you will let you become a very credible non-verbal communicator.

NON-VERBAL TIPS FOR YOUR COMMUNICATION STYLE

How You Prepare Information	
Meticulous	*Holistic*
What Likely Works for You	What Likely Works for You
You are not going to walk into a room to make a presentation and be surprised. You check out the room in advance. You note where people sit and what that says about the organization. You know who is in charge and you pay close attention to their non-verbal signals. Objectics is your sweet spot. Your slides are ready, you have backups to your backups. You check out the projector. Your thoroughness on these physical elements of non-verbal communication serves a dual purpose: it adds to your comfort level and communicates to your listeners that you have your act together.	Consummate winger that you are, you figure you will be comfortable no matter what the situation. Size of the room? No issue. Projector goes dark? No problem. People standing up or shuffling papers. No matter. This enables your own non-verbal communication to be relaxed, connected and useful in building your credibility with your audience.

What to Watch Out For	What to Watch Out For
Always remember that preparation is fine, but it is fallible. Be prepared that for all of your preparation, something will go wrong. When it does, let your non-verbal signals to your listeners demonstrate your poise and grace under pressure. Smile. Keep your face relaxed. No matter what you are feeling inside, keep it to yourself. This builds valuable credibility capital because it shows you are both good at preparation and comfortable under pressure.	A little attention in advance will not take away your spontaneity or big picture thinking. You can find your credibility taking a hit when flexibility becomes disorder, or worse, chaos. Try to avoid non-verbal errors. Know where the deciders sit and watch reactions. Make sure your visual aids actually aid understanding. Try to pull in what is often a kind of communication intensity that manifests itself in proximity to the listeners, random gestures and movement, or a failure to track the non-verbal signals your audience is always sending out. Any or all of these will likely impede building credibility capital because the audience is feeling overwhelmed. That is uncomfortable and tiring and your goals are likely to be the casualty.

How You Convey Information

Direct	*Diplomatic*
What Likely Works for You	What Likely Works for You
Confident in what you say, your non-verbal communication is likely to come across as focused. You make eye contact. You stick to your allowed time. You make sure your slides and materials are on point. So, your non-verbal communication is going to be content-focused.	You may not be thinking about your own non-verbal communication, but you are looking carefully at your audience and taking note of what they are communicating to you. Some of it may be unconscious, but you are taking in all of their signals. You are apt to use those signals to adjust your talk to ensure you are being clear and they are engaged.

What to Watch Out For	What to Watch Out For
You likely don't – but should – use non-verbal to help you connect to the audience on a more personal level. Let your facial expression relax, maybe even smile. Let your hands be at ease. This will allow your natural gestures to emerge. Carefully move around the room. This does not mean pace back and forth, it means don't stand like a statue in one place. Your listeners might not know why, but they will feel you are focused as much on them as you are on your content, thereby building credibility capital.	Your own non-verbal communication should, however, be something you think about when you begin. You are feeling connected to your audience, but make sure you do not stand too close to the front rows. Let your eyes roam around the room rather than focus on those who are with you or as may be your instinct, those who seem sceptical. Watch your time. You may find yourself working to respond to their non-verbal signals, but extemporaneously taking a tangent to try to address what you are seeing may take you down a path with no cheese at the end of it, thereby doing damage to your credibility capital.

How You Receive Communication

Relational	*Substantive*
What Likely Works for You	What Likely Works for You
You are pretty much always listener-focused. This means even if you don't realize it, you are all about the non-verbal communication, which is a major element of active listening. You may want to pay more conscious attention to your listeners' non-verbal cues, however. This will help move your reactions to them from reflexive to intentional.	You are focused on the content and how your listeners are absorbing it. So, when your audience members indicate, even non-verbally, that they have questions, you will pay attention. You may not notice the subtle hints, however. So, asking the audience for feedback by using statements such as 'Does that make sense?' might get you some more overt non-verbal responses like head nods.

What to Watch Out For	What to Watch Out For
In the midst of a talk, paying attention to the audience is important, but not at the expense of your content. Definitely use your audience's cues to determine what they are reacting to, their interest level, their understanding – but not to the detriment of accomplishing your goals. Do not lose your focus on what you prepared.	Remember, achieving your goals is inextricably connected to your audience's engagement as well as their understanding. If they are not engaged, you are not progressing on the objective journey. Master reading the room. You do this by paying close attention to those verbal cues. Since your natural tendency is to assume they are listening to you, the non-verbal cues are likely to be invisible. The best way to improve your mastery of the language of non-verbal cues is to practise. Do this outside of the presentation situation. Anytime you are with people, pay attention to their non-verbal cues. You may well find that your credibility capital increases in a number of areas of your life.

How You Relate to Others

Collaborative	*Independent*
What Likely Works for You	What Likely Works for You
You do not take relationships for granted. You are very aware that people are not always candid when issues arise. So, likely you have become fluent in non-verbal communication. This means that you are always reading the room to ensure your listeners are tracking. This enables you to sense issues, sometimes even before people realize they have them.	Laser-focused on your goals as you are, your unconscious non-verbal communication is apt to demonstrate it. Likely when you defend your arguments and make your points your voice is strong, eye contact direct, gestures controlled. This cues your listeners that you are confident in your approach and arguments.

What to Watch Out For	What to Watch Out For
Audience focus is important, but so too is achieving your goal. Watch out for a tendency to begin to make changes to your content in real time based on what you are sensing from the audience. Additionally, remember that you are sending out non-verbal cues all of the time. Empathetic as you are, you may be showing that you have more concern for what your listeners want than advocating for your position. So, work on that personal non-verbal balance. It will reap credibility capital rewards.	Your concentration on your stance on the topic may lead to ignoring non-verbal feedback from your audience. This is fraught with peril as it means you miss key information that can guide you as you proceed. Pay attention to them as you speak. Note when they fidget, write, look at their phones or change facial expressions. All of these signs can indicate agreement or opposition, preparing you for the discussion after your presentation, so pay attention to them.

Your Communication Personality

Animated	*Controlled*
What Likely Works for You	What Likely Works for You
You are non-verbal communication personified. Your facial expressions, gestures, body movement are all part of your natural communication arsenal. Your expressiveness is as much a part of your presentation as your slides are and tends to be natural and unconscious: you think it, you show it.	Chances are your photo is in the dictionary under poker face. You just don't let much show. This means that even when there is pushback, you don't react non-verbally. Your demeanour, gestures, vocal quality, body movement do not tend to reveal your inner thoughts. This requires people to pay close attention to your words as there aren't a lot of other signals.

What to Watch Out For	What to Watch Out For
While your animated personality can be a great asset, it can also create credibility issues if your listeners feel you are going over the top so make sure your non-verbal communication matches the tenor and tone of your topic. Rein it in when the topic demands a more low-key presentation such as cost reductions, schedules unmet and other kinds of serious topics. Ensure your non-verbal communication matches the situation.	Non-verbal communication can be a powerful persuasive force, but you may tend to leave this weapon firmly locked in our arsenal and unused. Letting the audience into your thoughts via non-verbal signals can be engaging. More importantly, you need to pay attention to the audience's non-verbal communication. You focus on your point of view and communicating that. This can mean you miss subtle but real non-verbal signals from your listeners so pay attention to what they reveal – it will enable you to determine which elements of your talk are resonating and which are not. Effectively responding to these signals will help build your credibility capital.

9

Agendas: Hidden and Otherwise

As you read in the foundational chapters, context is everything. Whether or not our communication is successful depends in large part on it. Making a conscious effort to understand that context is therefore invaluable. Fortunately, it's usually relatively straightforward to do so. Usually, but not always. There is, however, one subset of context that is less accessible and much trickier to navigate: hidden agendas.

Hidden agendas are the invisible and private priorities and goals of individuals with whom we are dealing. Sometimes these are merely a natural feature and complication of communication. Other times, and far more damaging, are those that are actively intended to disrupt or derail the process. These agendas can become one of the greatest communication credibility land mines of all, because they hold the key to your ability to reach or influence someone, yet they are never disclosed or openly discussed. That doesn't mean that everyone is malicious or villainous in their dealings, but they may have goals that run counter to your own and that may throw a spanner in your communication strategy as they go after their own objectives at the expense of yours.

Hidden agendas are integrally connected to credibility. In fact, the reason these personal agendas are hidden is usually because people know their own credibility would be at risk in a given context if their goals were fully transparent. You, in turn, can actually enhance your own credibility by understanding the hidden agendas of others: even if the individual on the other side of the table won't engage in good faith, your ability to recognize and navigate the unseen adds an important asset to your credibility capital with peers who observe your dexterity and skills.

Certainly, there are cases when agendas are actively hidden through deception or strategic omission but it's important to recognize that hidden agendas can also be subconscious – sometimes the agendas may hide even from the individuals themselves. That is to say they are just reacting in the moment by instinct, rather than working to a plan. As researchers McKay, Davis and Fanning suggest, agendas 'are excellent defensive maneuvers if you don't feel good about yourself. They protect you from rejection by creating the desired impression. Over and over, they help you make a case for your essential value as a person.'[1] In any case – whether or not it's a conscious strategy on their part to hide their agenda – it's safe to assume that pretty much everybody has a plan for themselves, for their families, for their careers. That plan creates a cocoon of context through which your credibility, as well as theirs, will be evaluated.

[1]McKay, Matthew, Davis, Martha & Fanning, Patrick (2009), *Messages: The Communication Skills Book*, 3rd ed, Oakland, CA: New Harbinger Publications, 80.

So, hidden agendas are not necessarily malicious, but they are inherently ambiguous and opaque. Consequently, the more you know about who you are communicating with and their motivations, the better able you are to navigate these often-treacherous credibility waters. Everyone's personal history is actually a roadmap to their hidden agendas. The more you understand about where they come from – literally and figuratively – the more tools you have to uncover and understand those agendas and the better chance you have to protect your interests and credibility.

Steven was preparing the gaming division president of a major entertainment conglomerate for his first presentation at a business retreat. This was the first retreat with the newly promoted CEO. As is often the case with shake-ups, the executive ranks were nervous about how the CEO's potential new direction and priorities might affect them. The gaming division had won some recent successes, but that did not ease anxieties about what the future might hold in this incredibly competitive and fickle industry. In order to successfully advocate for his division, the gaming division president had to understand the unspoken interests and objectives that would effectively secure the new CEO's support.

The CEO's hidden agenda turned out to be rather easy to uncover. A little research revealed his disdain for on-site virtual reality (VR) exhibits. This innovative but highly speculative aspect of gaming required a huge upfront investment of time and capital. The division president, focusing on building his credibility and making a good impression, demonstrated his vision for the sector. Aware of the preconceived notions of the new CEO, however, he was careful in his prioritizing and decided to de-emphasize VR attractions in the presentation. He did not leave out his plans, but he did minimize the importance of this area of growth to the ultimate success. When the presentation was over, many in the division were surprised by the low-key billing of VR – that is until they heard the CEO's closing remarks when he made no mention of VR as part of his immediate plans. Colleagues were impressed with the division president's read of the situation and subsequent adaptability, resulting in an increase in his credibility capital.

A classic mistake we all tend to make is to assume other people operate like we do and are impressed or put off by the same things as we are. In truth, most often our personal points of view probably don't mesh. What seems devastating to you might just be another day at the office for them, and vice versa. Add in the fact that a hidden agenda may make it more difficult to understand someone's personal matrix and you may miss critical indicators of what matters to them and why. Moving back to the roadmap analogy, everyone's agenda road is riddled with signposts indicating their intentions – you just have to be alert to them. Their choice of schools, jobs, office furnishings, cars, where they live, attire, work and business friends, parental activities are all revealing of personal priorities: What do they value and appreciate? What image of themselves are they trying to cultivate or project? In this sense, decoding interests requires a bit of detective work (similar, in fact, to figuring out the culture in an organization so you may want to revisit Chapter 3, Communication Culture, *see also* pp. 33–49, for more on deciphering the meaning in everyday symbols and codes). Understanding this gives you a more complete picture of a life's agenda.

WHAT TO LOOK OUT FOR

If you pay attention, people's hidden agendas become more apparent. It may take some time to determine what exactly the ultimate goal is, but the fact that there is one may not be so difficult to see. One common tell is that those with agendas tend to steer conversation towards themselves, focusing discussion on how the subject affects them directly. This isn't (necessarily) narcissism, but rather an effort to steer the issue towards their desired outcome. Even when the conversation moves on to seemingly unrelated matters, those with agendas will often bring the subject matter back to their priorities.

People with hidden agendas tend to be very invested in the outcome and work overtime to drive to it. This can result in oversized emotional reactions to even the smallest negative aspects of the subject. Generally, the greater the misplaced emotion, the more they are attached to the result and cannot but help to show their personal concerns about the outcome. Paraphrased from Shakespeare, the expression 'methinks he or she doth protests too much' comes to mind. Most people just aren't that good at being able to conceal their real perspectives and feelings. The key is to listen and watch.

There are also physical tells that someone may be concealing information or their full intentions. One of the most common physical indicators of hidden agendas is avoiding eye contact. At one point, there was a popular belief – helped along by a good dose of genius TV detectives who zero in on minute facial expressions to uncover some shocking truth – that the direction people looked indicated whether they were telling a lie or the truth. That might make for good TV, but research has fully and convincingly put that theory to rest. You simply cannot tell if someone is lying simply because they looked to the left or the right. In fact, you cannot even tell if they are lying if they look away from direct contact with you, no matter if it is up, down or sideways.[2] Research shows that eye contact is actually often just a signal of an internal war between words and actions, a battle of cognitive resources.[3] Both maintaining eye contact and searching for words or concepts require mental effort – and when the two are put in direct competition, eye contact usually loses out. Researchers Kajimura and Nomura studied this phenomenon, explaining that this competition 'generates an urge to break eye contact in order to facilitate verbal processing'.[4] So, be wary of putting too much weight into what is going on when someone breaks eye contact. As the saying goes, sometimes a cigar is just a cigar!

Paying attention to someone's eye movements won't make you a human lie detector. Still, in context, it can be a valuable clue that something is going on that's worth paying close attention to. So, what else might tip you off that hidden agendas are at play? Pay attention when someone out of the blue seems to be unusually and overly solicitous on learning your perspective on an issue. True, it is always flattering to be asked your opinion, the implication being that what you have to

[2] Wiseman, Richard et al. (11 July 2012), 'The Eyes Don't Have It: Lie Detection and Neuro-Linguistic Programming', *PLOS ONE* 7, No. 7: e40259, https://doi.org/10.1371/journal.pone.0040259

[3] Kajimura, Shogo & Nomura, Michio (1 December 2016), 'When We Cannot Speak: Eye Contact Disrupts Resources Available to Cognitive Control Processes during Verb Generation', *Cognition* 157: 352–57, https://doi.org/10.1016/j.cognition.2016.10.002

[4] Ibid.

say and think matters. Those with an agenda, however, may have an ulterior motive in play. Knowing that their own plans cannot survive in a vacuum, they will want to understand your perspectives on issues. They need allies to build consensus for their agenda, hidden though it might be; they want to know if you can fit into their plans. They also need to figure out if you are going to be part of the opposition and if so, whether your opinions can influence others.

HOW TO NAVIGATE SOMEONE'S HIDDEN AGENDA

Hidden agendas are ubiquitous. Managing them will enable you to manage the narrative and protect your own credibility. It's wise not to over-rely on what you will pick up by analysing a conversation in the moment. Forewarned is forearmed. Taking the time to figure out if there are hidden agendas at play will pay dividends. Be careful, however, as you do not want to be seen as working your own hidden agendas. This is not spying or being deceitful, it's uncovering the easily accessible soft data that makes you smarter and your messages clearer. It's what sociologist Erving Goffman referred to in his influential work, *The Presentation of Self*, as 'free' secrets.[5] A free secret, Goffman explains, is somebody else's secret that can be disclosed without undermining your own role and credibility. It's being observational without being deceptive, doing your homework before the big test. You should still be tactful about it though: while scheduling smaller meetings with some colleagues in advance may give you insight, it can also look like an attempt to bypass others on your part. Better to gather data informally, listening more than talking. That will give you a better understanding of the motivations in play.

In the midst of a hidden agenda struggle, you may find yourself having to fight fire with fire. One powerful rhetorical tool is the pivot. We see it all the time in the political realm, but it can also be an important survival device that can save your credibility in the business world. True, it's the art of the dodge, but more than that, it's a way

[5]Goffman, Erving (1959), *The Presentation of Self in Everyday Life*, Anchor Books edition. Garden City, N.Y.: Doubleday, https://search.library.wisc.edu/catalog/9994678047 02121

to make sure you are getting your message across. It's the art of not falling prey inadvertently to another's agenda; the pivot moves the conversational ball from their playground to yours.

A well-placed story can also effectively shift the conversation – often without others even realizing this has occurred. Of course, this tactic is not yours alone. It can be a race to see who can play the story card first and push the emotional buttons to achieve the desired reactions. A story can be used in a variety of positive ways, but it can also be a way to trigger more negative emotions such as guilt and embarrassment. Perhaps you had a project that did not work out as planned. A story about a different project but with the same unhappy outcome might make you feel targeted, resulting in embarrassment or humiliation. Stay focused and don't succumb. Use your stories to move the narrative arc more positively towards engagement and support. At the very least, pay attention so you are not caught off guard.

One of the best ways to stay credible to those with hidden agendas is to simplify your own offering. Like a bad game of Telephone or Whispers, something is almost always lost in translation and communication is especially likely to be misconstrued when you have to say something that doesn't fit into someone else's agenda. And while we shouldn't compromise our messaging entirely to satisfy the needs of others, the more we know about what simply 'pushes their buttons', the better the chance of achieving the desired effect. This is where you want to closely monitor your reactions. Your ability to focus on your most fundamental messaging will enable you to maintain credibility and avoid getting caught up in someone else's convoluted plans. As we said, those with hidden agendas are usually desperate to understand just how, or if, you will fit into their agendas. By not getting caught up in that double-think analysis, you maintain your credibility through clarity. This 'just the facts, Ma'am' approach may not make you a star in the moment, but it will keep you from being sucked into the vortex of an agenda from which you have no control. It's a big picture philosophy that will serve you well.

Speaking of keeping your own emotions and instincts in check, one of the most important aspects of dealing with those who have an agenda is to resist the urge to call them out. That can be quite the hazardous strategy and likely won't do anything to change either the agenda or the person. In fact, it is more likely to reveal your own concerns and vulnerabilities. Your job, then, is just to understand, communicate and maintain your focus. You do not need to conquer them, just work with them.

Keeping a keen eye on those with suspected hidden agendas is the best way to decide how to be the most effective communicator and take the best course of action. The best indicator of whether you are falling victim to someone else's agenda is if you don't feel right about a conversation. Call it intuition or your own version of Spider-Man's 'Spidey-sense', but it's actually your choice whether to be caught in their web or not.

AGENDAS: TIPS FOR YOUR COMMUNICATION STYLE

How You Prepare Information	
Meticulous	*Holistic*
What Likely Works for You	What Likely Works for You
As you delve into your planning, you are likely to think about what others are thinking and planning themselves. Make sure you look back over recent history to identify the clues as to what others might be formulating. As you start thinking about this, pay close attention to informal communication interactions as well as more formal meetings and the like. This can give you valuable insights.	You look beyond the obvious and this can give you early notice that there are hidden agendas at play. Your ability to think on your feet can help you adjust as covert agendas see the light of day. Not being wedded to a particular approach can give you a way to forge alliances and achieve your goals, hidden agendas or not.
What to Watch Out For	What to Watch Out For
The more concerned you become about hidden agendas, the more planning you may feel you have to do. Certainly, think and plan. Do not, however, become mired in planning to the extent that you feel unprepared to move into action. Analysis paralysis is real and you want to keep moving forward.	This would be a good time to take a page out of your meticulous colleague's playbook. Don't wait for the next meeting to think about the ramifications of that hidden agenda. What might their plan mean for what you are trying to achieve? It's even more important to think about this if the hidden agenda is the boss or decision maker. Do a little bit of sleuthing and you may find yourself in a strong position to put your impromptu communication skills to work.

How You Convey Information	
Direct	*Diplomatic*
What Likely Works for You	What Likely Works for You
Your tendency to go directly to the heart of the matter can cut through many a hidden agenda. You are going to call them as you see them. This can enable covert agendas to see the light of day, resulting in more open dialogue.	You approach people and issues with an eye towards how they will react, so when you sense a hidden agenda in play, you are not going to jump right in and call it out. It might result in embarrassment, which would not move discussions forward.
What to Watch Out For	What to Watch Out For
Sometimes calling out those unseen agendas does not result in more clarity but less. There was a reason that agenda was hidden and bringing it out into the open can lead to conflict. Directness is sometimes best used with a light touch and subtlety. You will find this is the path to build credibility capital.	Sometimes letting something go is not the best strategy, even if doing the opposite is uncomfortable. An unwillingness to identify and address a hidden agenda often plays out to your disadvantage. A hidden agenda ignored is a hidden agenda that wins. You do not have to address it in an uncomfortably direct manner but doing so in your inimitable diplomatic style will lead to a more desirable outcome and in turn increase your credibility capital.

How You Receive Communication	
Relational	*Substantive*
What Likely Works for You	What Likely Works for You
You pay close attention to what people say and how they say it. Perhaps even more importantly when looking at hidden agendas is your propensity to see how others are receiving communication, not just yourself. This helps you gauge whether the hidden agendas are recognized as well as where there might be support or opposition and can give insight others might not possess.	You are almost always going to focus on the 'what' rather than the 'who' in communication. You are listening for anything and everything that might threaten your goals and objectives. This can enable you to catch a hidden agenda almost before it has become fully formed.

What to Watch Out For	What to Watch Out For
Focusing on people is important, but do not let it get in the way of evaluating the essence of the agenda content. You want to stay connected to your goals. Make sure you do not get caught up in others' reactions at the expense of what you want to accomplish.	There are two potential landmines you want to watch out for. First, if the discussion heads in a direction you do not think connects or is of interest, you might tune out and miss key relevant information. Second, you might overlook key signals people give off that are separate from the specifics of their plan but indicate their concealed goals. Integrating the content and the people will serve you well.
How You Relate to Others	
Collaborative	*Independent*
What Likely Works for You	What Likely Works for You
Your connection to people is important to you. You bank on it to ease your way with others. Building relationships is your stock in trade and this can help you identify those who are not as forthcoming as you expect.	You are willing to engage with others, even if it requires a little bit of conflict. This means if you identify a hidden agenda, you are unlikely to ignore it. This is especially true if you feel the hidden agenda takes aim at your goals and purposes, but any hidden agenda is likely to be fair game.
What to Watch Out For	What to Watch Out For
You might be forgiven for thinking everyone is as collaborative as you are, but, alas, they are not. Make sure you pay attention to what might be going on below the surface. Others may take advantage of your collaborative nature and use you to drive towards a consensus focused on their hidden agenda. Stay connected to your goals, it will help build your credibility capital.	As you are focused more on the 'what' than the 'who', you risk losing potential allies early on. Don't be so quick to out someone's concealed agenda if it will engender sympathy at your expense. Work on building some connection with people even as you identify the hidden agendas at play. Focusing on the content only and how that impacts your goals can make you look selfish and self-serving. That is sure to deplete your credibility capital.

Your Communication Personality

Animated	*Controlled*
What Likely Works for You	**What Likely Works for You**
Your vivid style is without doubt a major component of your persuasiveness. People are drawn into your orbit and will most likely find themselves agreeing with your perspective. When you see a hidden agenda at play, you can often secure others' agreement and support.	Your calm demeanour enables you to keep any concerns about hidden agendas to yourself. Even when those covert plans are beginning to make themselves known, your demeanour conveys unconcern. This enables you to start identifying the areas most damaging to your interests and begin to marshal your forces in defence of your interests.
What to Watch Out For	**What to Watch Out For**
You have a lot going for you, but that easy-to-read style means that subtlety may be your lost art. When a hidden agenda reveals itself, it may be difficult for you to keep that information to yourself while you determine the best course of action. The good news is that since your reputation is one of expressiveness, when you can keep something to yourself, people will not wonder if there is something you are not sharing. This gives you time to gather more information and plan a strategy to support your goals in the face of hidden opposition.	You want to make certain your seeming unconcern does not derail you. People may assume either you do not care, or you are not even aware of others' Machiavellian moves. Make sure you pay attention to potential allies to assess where they stand. Don't assume that the best way to deal with hidden agendas is to ignore them and assume others will as well – concealed agendas do not mean harmless.

10

Meetings, Bloody Meetings

If Gallup ever decides to poll people about their feelings about meetings, it may be the first poll in history to have nigh on 100 per cent agreement on anything. People just tend to feel that meetings are generally a waste of time. They are also expensive, with the cost of poorly organized meetings in 2019 alone reaching $399 billion (£300 billion) in the US and $58 billion (£44 billion) in the UK.[1]

And yet meetings remain an unyielding fact of organizational life and success in meetings often equals broader career success. So, if you can understand meeting dynamics and corral them effectively, you can turn them into major opportunities.

As with interviews and presentations, meetings are an opportunity for you to take centre stage and present yourself and your message in the most effective way possible. Never take a meeting, however routine, for granted. Go into every meeting with a purpose; if you are not focused on that purpose, then it is a missed opportunity at best, a waste of time at worst. The more strategic your approach to the meeting, and the more clearly you define its purpose and your goal, the more likely you will achieve your desired outcome.

Whether you're a presenter or participant in a meeting, just 'winging it' and trusting in spontaneity and luck is a risky strategy. True, you may be able to pull it off 10 per cent of the time, but that is a pretty low success rate and the negative results could haunt you, and your career, for years. In business, bad memories are long. Mistakes follow you much longer than your successes do. If you think this is meant to scare you, then you are right. Every meeting is an opportunity for things to go right, or terribly wrong. Understanding your place, your opportunities, and the context in which those opportunities occur is vital.

MEETING LEADERS AND PRESENTERS

Productive meetings require planning, thought and care. If you are in the position to run a meeting, take it as an opportunity to demonstrate your leadership and communication skills. The key elements for a successful meeting are: 1) setting a clear agenda; 2) effectively reading the room and 3) assessing meeting context.

The Agenda
Prior to the meeting, think long and hard about your agenda. This means more than just developing your notes and slides. If you have

[1]Economy, Peter, 'A New Study of 19 Million Meetings Reveals That Meetings Waste More Time Than Ever' (but There Is a Solution), (2019) Inc.com.

called the meeting, your agenda should offer an overall timeline and breakdown of topics to be covered. Share it with participants, ideally in advance, so that everyone comes to the meeting with a shared understanding of its purpose and goal. That also means that you need to make sure that you stick to the plan as much as possible: attendees will be following your agenda and it will increase your credibility when they see organizational discipline. Structurally, identify whether there are to be introductions, question and answer sessions, collaborative discussion, decisions and how those decisions will be made. That is how you will achieve real and perceived control in moving discussion forward. What the participants actually retain from the meeting is dependent upon follow-up, but having a commanding presence and a credible platform are the most essential, tangible takeaways that you can control.

Your agenda is more than the timeline. You will want to think of a meeting as a series of conversations. Design the conversations in your mind ahead of time. If the meeting is particularly important, rehearse where you can. Absolutely rehearse the written or bullet-pointed script of your presentation, but also think through the discussion session and have responses ready for likely questions. It helps to seek out allies who will give you open and honest feedback as you prepare and rehearse. Roleplay. Let the potential obstacles and second-guessing resistance come out in a safe environment so you can address them in advance. Better to find the holes in your argument when you have the chance to do something about it. The stars never magically align during the actual meeting presentation such that you win your case. Seek out those who don't have a stake in the outcome or a position to defend; they will be your best sounding boards because their objectivity isn't encumbered.

The most important element in a meeting, particularly one that is focused on gaining consensus or a decision, is the discussion, whether that's a formal question and answer session or less structured conversation throughout the meeting. This is where you find out what your audience is thinking about your message and where they are ready to push back. Think about those hard questions – the ones you hope no one will ever ask. If you know there will be someone in the room, all too often a superior or decision maker, who has already revealed an opposing or sceptical perspective, identify the basis for that opinion and formulate your responses accordingly. You might want to pre-empt some of those arguments in your presentation, but it is unlikely that you will change their minds doing that alone. So, you will want to prepare for the rebuttals that come in the shape of Q&A. Marshall your evidence and craft your answers. Think about how to refute opposing arguments without making it personal. Try to understand the naysayer's perspective and know there may be others in the room who will want to take advantage of the opportunity at your expense. Don't rely on others to come to your aid – this is *your* meeting.

Rehearsing will add to your preparation, but don't expect the meeting to necessarily proceed as planned. If you do, the first time something happens you did not foresee, you may well lose your mental footing. Rehearsing will, however, give you more mastery over your material and your arguments so that you can quickly recover.

You can do all of this most effectively if you are being focused and observational, but you can't be observational and pick up on the context of how you are being received unless you are comfortable enough with the material you are presenting. Only then can you allow yourself to absorb the feedback and the mood of the room. This is referred to as 'reading the room'.

Reading the Room

The *Farlex Dictionary of Idioms* defines reading the room as 'understand[ing] the emotions and thoughts of the people in the room'.[2] You must use all of your senses and a bit of intuition to get a sense of the mood in the room. See what is happening in the room. Who is sitting next to whom? To whom are they talking? Listen as best you can to what is being said and how. You may not be able to pick up all the words, but you can definitely get a sense of the feelings. What are the expressions on people's faces? Rooms have energy. In the best situations, when people are engaged, the participants actually feed energy to the presenter and vice versa.

---

[2]'Read the Room', *Farlex Dictionary of Idioms*, 2015, https://idioms.thefreedictionary.com/read+the+room

When there is little or no energy, the room can suck the enthusiasm out of the presenter and material being presented can come off as dry. Sense the energy in the room. If it is high, feed on it; if low, you'll just need to put out more.

Reading the room, and understanding the context in which information is presented, can give you an extra boost in a meeting that may also help you combat nervousness. If you feel that the room is on your side, you will likely feel less judged and therefore able to be more relaxed and conversational. You can sense where the alliances are and in what direction they lean; you can intuitively sense where there might be support. All of this adds to your ability to achieve your strategic objective and follow through on your stated agenda.

Assessing Meeting Context
The truth is, however, nothing takes place in a vacuum and organizational meetings are no different. Context matters. You want to ensure you know what other external and internal factors are in play that could impact your meeting. In the military, this is known as Situational Analysis and it has saved many a campaign. Often referred to by the acronym PMESII (Political, Military, Economic, Social, Information, Infrastructure) in military parlance, for you it is more likely to be Political, Management, Employees, Spreadsheets, Information and Infrastructure.

Politics are always in play. So, what are the political machinations facing your project? Who is jockeying for position over whom? What are the stressors on management? This can be executive or program management – what are the pressure points there? All too often employees are an ignored factor in situational analysis. Employee morale should always be considered. Make sure there are no staffing issues in the works that could affect your plan. Spreadsheets are always going to be a major issue because, let's face it, everything eventually comes down to the bottom line and money in some fashion. What is the financial situation of the organization? What are the economic factors in the country? In the world? Lean times call for different strategies and tactics than in prosperous ones. Information is always power, so don't skimp on gathering it. Look for sources from whom you might not ordinarily hear. Cast that information net widely.

Infrastructure matters internally and externally. What equipment will you need? What space? What software? What tools? As the world goes more and more digital and virtual, make sure you have the infrastructure resources required.

When presenting within your own organization, you should be able to identify these PMESII elements relatively easily but don't ignore what is happening elsewhere in your organization that might impact what you are looking to achieve. Yes, you know the players and their history. You may even know their positions on the matter at hand. Just don't forget that Situational Analysis means looking at context beyond the conference room's four walls. Your division might be having a profitable quarter, but a different one may have just lost a major contract to a competitor. Their difficulty might impact your ability to take advantage of your quarterly success.

A lot of meetings, sales presentations, pitches and customer reviews, for example, take place outside of your own organization. All the same PMESII rules apply here, so do your homework. Make sure you are as knowledgeable as possible about the attendees. You will have prepared for the meeting, but events move fast so make sure you do a day-before Google search of the participants and their businesses. The stock might have taken a hit. There might have been a press release for a new venture. An executive might have given an interview. Make sure you know about them. Also, look broadly using your PMESII tools. If there is something else going on regarding trends in the news, even though nonspecific, it might have an impact on the mood of those in attendance. You have no excuse not to know what it is. It may be no more than gossip and there may be unattainable X factors to consider, but since that is one of the currencies businesses run on, it's as real as the truth in that moment.

MEETING ATTENDEES

Whether you are aware of it or not, people take on distinct roles in a meeting. Participants tend to fall into one of the following roles: *Instigator, Bystander, Confronter, Facilitator* and *Spectator*. Certainly, this is not an exhaustive list, and these are general classifications which may go by other similar names, but research suggests these five types of roles show up most frequently. As a participant, considering which role you choose, or chooses you, will colour how your contributions to a meeting are perceived by others. By the same token, being aware of these roles as a meeting leader will help you manage the meeting and assess how your goals are progressing.

An *Instigator* is the person promoting a new idea or thought. Sometimes an *Instigator* will provide support by refuting opposition or by providing a new perspective or argument. An *Instigator* can also be someone who presents a new, often opposing, idea or thought.

A *Bystander* will latch onto someone else's idea by agreeing with it. If they express support for your position, try to understand what is beneath the agreement. It could well be just what it seems to be – you persuaded them that this is the right approach and they are publicly expressing that support. That is not to say you should always take that support at face value. If you did your homework, you should be able to estimate if the support is real or a play in a longer game for them. The *Bystander* may also support positions opposing yours, so pay attention to any subtext.

Confronters are arrayed against your argument. Those attendees who are open about their opposition and express their reservations are to be welcome. This allows you to address and refute their arguments. Certainly, we prefer agreement, but adversaries who let us know where they stand are a good second. The group to be wary of are the confronters, who keep their own counsel. They may be biding their time, they may be working behind your back. Pay attention to insinuations, inflections and undertones.

The *Facilitator* works to ensure all participants can share their thoughts and that the meeting process is effective. A facilitative meeting attendee pays close attention to the tenor of the conversation and works to keep tensions low. *Facilitators* will often ask questions of participants just to elicit perspectives. A facilitative participant is a valuable contributor to any meeting, but they can be rare. Some organizations have assigned *Facilitators* to meetings. These people focus on the meeting process rather than the content.

The *Spectator* is decidedly non-committal. A *Spectator* turns over thought to the other attendees occasionally by asking other's opinions. Be very wary and very strategic if you find yourself taking this role.

Very few meetings offer you the luxury of playing only one of these roles and you will be most successful if you can move casually and seamlessly from one position to another. If you are dealing with a fierce *Confronter*, you may want to start by being a *Spectator* – don't begin an argument you can't win. Acknowledge the opposition related to how it might affect the group, but then seek to understand the why behind the negativity. Become a *Facilitator*. Try to suss out what is behind their opposition. Ask probing questions. Listen to the answers before diving in with what might be perceived as defensive answers. There may be a hidden agenda at play.

Unless you really don't have strong opinions on the topic or you know exactly what the response will be, playing the role of a bystander can be counterproductive if your goal is to give the appearance of a forward-thinking employee.

There may be concern over allocation of resources. There might even be a power play going on in another arena that is slopping over into your meeting. Once you have a better understanding, you can consider how you can address their concerns as a *Bystander*. This is probably the hardest role to take on in this situation because you need to come across as authentically interested in managing the discontinuity in the meeting. Work here to segue back to the original, or modified, idea so that you can move back into the *Instigator* role and focus on by making the point why it's important not to lose momentum, even if your original point has been adjusted to consider some or all of the opposition arguments.

COLLABORATION IN MEETINGS

One of the best ways to encourage collaboration in a meeting is to be sure the agenda is shared with the attendees in advance, especially if you think there might be opposition. Live, real-time collaboration is not everyone's strength. As Susan Cain states in her book, *Quiet: The Power of Introverts in a World That Can't Stop Talking*, 'we've come to overvalue all group work at the expense of solo thought.'[3] Good

---

[3]Cain, Susan (2013), *Quiet: The Power of Introverts in a World That Can't Stop Talking*, New York: Broadway Books.

leaders know this and take the time to set up team members for success by assigning collaborator lieutenants to give some structure to the collaboration process. Remember, the goal is to get the best and brightest out of everyone in a meeting, not to provide threatening obstacles for those afraid to speak out in a meeting environment.

All too often, organizations promote competition rather than collaboration between people or units. This is usually based in a belief that competition hones the best and the brightest. If you find yourself in a predetermined competitive meeting environment, a more co-operative approach can be your most powerful tool. This applies whether you are presenting or participating as a member of the group. Fostering a team-collaboration dynamic in a group setting is almost always a winning strategy. Don't be intimidated and let others isolate you.

Whether you are a presenter or attendee, your job in every meeting is not only to get out of it what you intended to accomplish in the immediate term, but to advance your long-term career goals as well. You need to be just as focused on your desired outcome and your role as a collaborator will have a definite impact on how you are perceived in a meeting. You probably already have your position on most issues, so this is not the place to try to impress by appearing to stage a meeting mutiny. Always think big picture. Don't worry about the fleeting high of the moment when others tell you what an excellent job you did in the meeting. Focus on what can be accomplished that will keep the project on track and yield the best reflection on you. Your long-term impact is the best reward.

Some of the most consistent data available on the subject of collaboration suggests it all comes down to three elements. Clear expectation of goals. A consistent incentive system for participation. Providing an environment for everyone's success. Compromising on any of these three pillars may offer an opportunity for grandstanding, but doesn't accomplish the ultimate, beneficial goals of a productive meeting.

If there are conflicting goals for a meeting, then collaboration is hobbled from the start. The push and pull of competition works against partnership. Whether you are meeting a leader, a presenter or an attendee, pay attention to the stated goal. Listen for the undertone that indicates an opposing goal. Ask for clarification of the goal if you are an attendee. Ask for input from the group around the goal if you are the leader. And, if you are the presenter, restate your goal to ensure everyone is on the same page.

Incentives for collaborating in meetings are usually intrinsic – face it, people are not paid to actively participate in a meeting. There are other kinds of factors that motivate them to engage beyond simply showing up at the scheduled time. Some people are motivated by visibility and the chance to interact with higher ups, others by increased recognition and accolades, still more by a sense of belonging. If you are the leader, understanding the variety of intrinsic incentives at play enables you to encourage collaboration. If you are a presenter or a participant, reading the room may give you the hints you need to guide the group into a collaborative environment.

Creating a collaborative environment is best done by a leader who both sets an example of co-operation and reinforces that kind of behaviour in participants. Interrupting negative discussion, encouraging people to speak to the present situation rather than dredge up past offences and focusing on constructive arguments can all reinforce collaboration. A presenter has a role in creating a participatory atmosphere by staying cool and calm, looking for points of agreement and generally taking on the role of collaborator-in-chief.

MEETINGS IN CRISIS

A meeting that has spiralled out of control is a meeting in crisis. This is not necessarily a meeting about an organizational crisis, rather, it is a meeting in which people's tempers have become frayed, stress overcomes strategy, people stop thinking and start reacting, and voices become louder as arguments become weaker. It's a true breakdown in communication. In these cases, people default to less thoughtful, and often irrational, forms of communication. Some power-oriented people kick into passion mode with terms like 'I need' or 'we must'. Participants may start arguing among themselves. They will often start to tell stories about how in the past they were ill-treated or how a project was torpedoed. Once the meeting has gone off the rails like this, it can be hard to get it back on track. Hard, but not impossible.

How can you best manage this kind of meeting crisis? This is where the *Facilitator* role is most valuable. And almost anyone can adopt a *Facilitator* role. Just encourage people to express their issues and concerns. Seek to keep the conversation on topic if you see one of the participants engaging in a takeover attempt. If you are the leader/ presenter, do not be dismissive of those expressing dissent. Yes, focus is important, but so too is demonstrating that you are aware of the immediate concerns being expressed. Tensions are only diffused when people believe they have been heard.

You must do all of this carefully. People are willing to be pulled back to the topic at hand, but not if they feel bullied or that their concerns are being ignored. Be wary of how you manage those trying to dominate in a meeting crisis – you do not want to win the battle and lose the war. As the presenter, this may all feel unsatisfying – after all, you wanted the conversation to focus on your presentation. If you are the leader, this can feel like you lost the meeting to chaos. But once people become engaged in shadow side issues, emotions take over. People need space and time to identify what happened and why. So, take a breath. Call a break. And when the group regathers, set the expectations once again.

If you find that the meeting agenda and logic have gone out the window, and the tactics described above aren't getting it back on track, now is the time to pull back on introducing any new concepts or suggestions that you want to see survive. Ideas introduced in a toxic atmosphere may die not because they are bad, but simply because they are associated with a negative environment. There will always be another meeting, but for you there's only one chance to introduce an idea and make a good first impression.

Meetings aren't going away. There are good meetings, bad meetings and truly ugly meetings. Railing against them as a frustrating, useless waste of time is akin to Mark Twain's observation on people and the weather: 'Everybody complains about it, but no one does anything to change it.' Weather cannot be changed, but meetings can. Be strategic. Have a plan. Listen. Read the room. Do this and you might just find that you can turn your meetings into a competitive advantage.

MEETING TIPS FOR YOUR
COMMUNICATION STYLE

How You Prepare Information

Meticulous	*Holistic*
What Likely Works for You	What Likely Works for You
You are likely to have an agenda for any meeting you attend, even if the meeting wasn't called by you. This primes your rhetorical pump to advocate for and defend your position. Just remember not to wait too long to dive into the discussion. Being a spectator while you wait for the perfect time is rarely a useful strategy, there is rarely a perfect time.	You look at the forest rather than the trees and in a meeting that can be a good way to make sure things stay on the right path. Meetings have a way of spiralling down tangents as people focus on one slide or one bullet point. Watch for the instigators. Their new ideas may be good, but they may not be timely. You can, and should, be on the lookout for these tangential discussions and remind people to get back to the heart of the matter. This makes the meeting much more efficient and effective, not to mention adding to your credibility capital.
What to Watch Out For	What to Watch Out For
As you sit in the meeting, remember to pay attention to what is going on around you. Your tendency to think about what you are going to say and how you are going to say it can mean you are not really present. You may be preparing to speak on a topic the group left five minutes ago, so stay in the moment!	When you aren't focused on the forest, however, you, too, can digress into brainstorming when it is time to move to a decision. There is a time for letting brains run free and there is a time to remember the forest. Don't confuse them.

How You Convey Information

Direct	*Diplomatic*
What Likely Works for You	What Likely Works for You
Your emphatic and often forceful style can give you a lot of leverage in meetings. People will almost have to listen to you. If you have thought through in advance what you want out of the meeting, your self-assured approach can reap great dividends.	You can be an effective facilitator in a meeting as you pay close attention to how people are reacting to each other, both in terms of content and interpersonally. You can help find areas of agreement and sort out the root issues of differences. You make meetings more productive when you take on this role.

What to Watch Out For	What to Watch Out For
Focused as you are on your point of view, you may miss key indicators of how the rest of the meeting attendees are reacting. Try to pay at least a little attention to how your points are being received. That will enable you to adapt if others are not buying what you are selling.	All well and good to be the grease that makes the meeting wheels go smoothly, but you don't want to forget that you have a stake in the discussion and decisions. So, step out of the facilitator role when you find your ideas getting stepped on!

How You Receive Communication

Relational	*Substantive*
What Likely Works for You	What Likely Works for You
Having someone in a meeting who is tuned in to the perceptions of attendees helps make the meeting go more smoothly. You can take on the facilitator role easily and when you do, all attendees are the better for it. What makes your approach unique, however, is your ability to sense the intrinsic motivators at play. By paying attention to perceptions, you can figure out what are the driving factors involved. Making these as apparent to others as they are to you will make the meeting more productive and more pleasurable for all.	You have focus and that is something meetings always need. While unlikely to be facilitative, you can take on leadership roles when the discussion needs focus. You can move the discussion to content when emotions threaten to take over.
What to Watch Out For	What to Watch Out For
For anyone taking on the unofficial facilitator role, the challenge becomes to keep your eye on your perspective ball. Efficient and productive is all well and good but not at the expense of your goals and objectives.	Pay attention! Yes, they may be discussing an issue or topic you don't care about, but you never know what that discussion portends for you and your goals. Meetings can move fast and if you are not paying attention, a decision might be made that really does impact you.

How You Relate to Others

Collaborative	*Independent*
What Likely Works for You	What Likely Works for You
Your natural instinct is to drive towards consensus and that is what you bring to the meeting table. People are probably used to seeing you in that role and so will tend to listen as you work to parse the various perspectives.	You aren't afraid to mix it up a bit so when there needs to be a little pushback, you are likely to be the one doing the pushing. Standing up for yourself and your ideas comes naturally to you. Just make sure you bring some tact to the discussion.

What to Watch Out For	What to Watch Out For
Your challenge is going to be to make use of all of that goodwill to further your own aims. You have to be willing to risk displeasing people so that you can accomplish your aims. Don't worry, you are hardwired to be sensitive to others so when you make your points, you are unlikely to consciously drive discord. Keep that balance and you will find your credibility capital soars.	Pay attention to how people are reacting to you when you decide to throw your hand grenade of disagreement onto the conference room table. You may think you are defending, but to others it may look as though you are derailing. Worse, given your well-deserved reputation of not being conflict avoidant, people may find themselves feeling defensive when you begin to talk. This means they are in their heads and not really listening. So, be gentle, be a bit mellow. Remember, you catch more flies with honey than with the vinegar of discord.

Your Communication Personality

Animated	*Controlled*
What Likely Works for You	What Likely Works for You
Energetic and dynamic, you can get almost anyone's attention. You can enliven the proceedings just by being yourself. As long as you match the tenor of the meeting, this can work well for you. Wouldn't hurt to take some of that pizzazz and use it to facilitate when tempers fray. That will definitely build your credibility capital!	Your measured style can bring emotions down when they start to run amuck. The challenge for you is to do this even in larger groups. Don't underestimate the impact your restrained approach to communication can have when people are starting to get exercised. Just be willing to engage. You can bring a great deal of value if you are willing to do it.
What to Watch Out For	What to Watch Out For
Your natural instinct is to lead, but there are times you can get more of what you want by being more of a follower. Think about gaining allies and letting them take the lead occasionally. You don't want to let your style overwhelm your substance.	Don't hide out! You may find yourself feeling overwhelmed when your more animated colleagues take to the stage. Sometimes you just need to ignore your internal instincts. As Rudyard Kipling noted, 'If you can keep your head when all about you are losing theirs ... Yours is the Earth and everything that's in it.'[4]

[4]Kipling, R. (1954). *Rudyard Kipling's verse: Definitive edition*. London: Hodder and Stoughton.

11

Conflict

Just the word 'conflict' is enough to give many people heart palpitations. It carries the connotations of discomfort, aggression, a fight in which there are few winners and lots of losers. In truth, conflict can be healthy for both organizations and individuals, as counterintuitive as that may seem.

Organizations are made up of people and people do not always agree. They have different perspectives, ideas, approaches, agendas and values.

Ironically, it is out of the crucible of conflict that organizations grow, innovations develop and better decisions are made. So, being able to manage conflict effectively is a critical credibility success factor. Inherent in effective management of conflict is tolerance for disagreement.

Ironically, people tend to manage conflict communication differently in their personal lives than they do in the workplace. If you know that you have to tell your spouse or significant other something that they are not going to like, you will probably think about how you can mitigate the upset this announcement could trigger. You do not walk through the door and drop the verbal bombshell. You think about the potential for disagreement, the reasons and the causes and try to find a way to navigate the conflict shoals, sometimes more successfully than others.

In organizational life there are myriad ways for conflict to rear its prickly head. Thinking about disagreements and conflict in organizations, how you engage with it and using effective techniques to manage it will build your communication skills and add to your credibility capital.

There is a difference between disagreement and conflict. McCroskey & Wheeless (1976) distinguish between *disagreement*, which relates to a difference of opinion on an issue, and *conflict*, which is more about personal characteristics and judgements.[1] That is to say, all disagreements do not necessarily devolve into conflict. Nauman suggests that conflict emerges from disagreement because 'of the low threshold of an individual to deal with anything that goes against their views'.[2] Managing yourself in a disagreement creates the possibility that it won't become a conflict damaging to both the organization and you.

Angouri & Locher suggest disagreement is an a priori part of human existence.[3] It makes sense given that we each interpret actions, words and

[1]Wheeless, Lawrence & McCroskey, James (1976), *Introduction to Human Communication*, Allyn & Bacon.
[2]Nauman, Saima (5 January 2018), 'Relationship of Tolerance for Disagreement with Conflict Management Styles', *Peshawar Journal of Psychology and Behavioural Sciences (PJPBS)* 3, No. 2: 145–64, https://doi.org/10.32879/pjpbs.2017.3.2.145-164
[3]Angouri, Jo & Locher, Miriam A. (1 September 2012), 'Theorising Disagreement', *Journal of Pragmatics*, 44, No. 12: 1549–53, https://doi.org/10.1016/j.pragma.2012.06.011

images according to our own perceptions, perspectives and experiences. Try making it through a day without disagreeing with something and someone. You may not voice your opposition, but it is there, lurking in the background and may eventually spring out like Athena from Zeus's brain. Human disagreement and subsequent conflict are, after all, the stuff of which movies, plays and books are made.

A wishful view of organizational conflict and disagreement is that these are an interruption to the natural state of things in which we live more in agreement than divergence. Scholars disagree.[4] Whether allocating resources or determining which proposal to accept or undertaking change efforts, the modern organization is rife with opportunities for disagreement and conflict.

The sheer ubiquity of disagreement enables a kind of cloak of invisibility in that we sometimes do not classify an interaction as disagreement. We might feel annoyed with something someone suggests and although we respond, we don't necessarily think of it as a disagreement ... yet. As the issue evolves, we may start to feel that we are losing something and then things begin to change. There are levels of disagreement that determine the intensity of our reactions and whether it becomes a conflict. One thing is true, however: avoiding engaging in disagreement for fear of conflict is almost always a failed strategy.

A clear sign of poor management is when an organization knowingly allows disagreement to become conflict. Researchers confirm that this affects organizations' productivity as well as employee satisfaction.[5] Martin Freres suggests that 'Workplace conflict appears to waste approximately 3 hours per week per employee [and] be directly related to costly turnover.'[6] The good news is the opposite is true as well. When disagreement and conflict are approached with effective

[4]Putnam, Linda L. (2013), 'Definitions and Approaches to Conflict and Communication', in *The SAGE Handbook of Conflict Communication*, 2nd ed., Thousand Oaks: SAGE Publications, Inc., 1–40, https://doi.org/10.4135/9781452281988

[5]Kay, Adam A. & Skarlicki, Daniel P. (July 2020), 'Cultivating a Conflict-Positive Workplace: How Mindfulness Facilitates Constructive Conflict Management', *Organizational Behaviour and Human Decision Processes* 159: 8–20, https://doi.org/10.1016/j.obhdp.2020.02.005

[6]Freres, Martin, *Journal of the International Ombudsman Association*. 2013, Vol. 6 Issue 2, p83–94. 12p.

communication, employees are more engaged with the organization and with each other.[7] In short, the goal should not be to eliminate disagreement but rather to keep it from degenerating into conflict.

MANAGING CONFLICT

Reducing conflict requires three approaches to disagreements: A tolerance for disagreement, separating the content from the personal and being willing to compromise. These are often tied to the personality traits of those involved and can be nurtured and consciously used. You can react competitively, emotionally and/or angrily when faced with disagreement, creating conflict. No matter how your organization tries to manage conflict, your approach is up to you. Management will always look to you to approach it collaboratively and deliberately, focusing on finding consensus rather than conflict.

TOLERANCE FOR DISAGREEMENT

There is an Aesop's fable about a group of mice who lived in terror of the local cat. They decided that if they put a bell on the cat, the sound would warn them. Then, they could scurry back to their hole in safety. Great idea, right? Except none of the mice was willing to approach the cat and attach the bell. Disagreements are a lot like Aesop's cat. Left alone, they can be a threat to organizational and career life and limb. Addressed, they sound alarms of potential issues that can be addressed and diffused. So, when there is discord, be the one who will bell the cat.

Tension is created when points of view diverge, no matter the issue, the cause or the nature of the controversy. People handle that tension differently. Some retreat, avoiding the strain and pressure of addressing it directly. They run the risk of developing a reputation for conflict escapism thus reducing both their credibility capital and trust. Some welcome the diversion of discord, seeing it as a kind of scorched earth tactic in which they emerge unscathed and triumphant. Others

---

[7]Tjosvold, Dean et al. (2008), 'Social Interdependence and Orientation Toward Life and Work1', *Journal of Applied Social Psychology* 38, No. 2: 409–35, https://doi.org/10.1111/j.1559-1816.2007.00311.x

step into the fray with alacrity, willing to engage and find collaborative solutions, approaches and consensus.

Conflict and disagreement avoidance have a number of causes. If you grew up in a home where disagreements were not aired but kept inside, you may lack the communication skills and comfort level to address them in the workplace. People who are reticent, quiet and introverted can feel a kind of emotional paralysis when confronted with the most benign of difference of opinion. Some people are reticent, unsure, perhaps introverted to the point where it is actually painful to confront opposition. Still more just prefer harmony, reasoning the negatives that could be created out of a skirmish are worse than ignoring the issue.

If you find yourself avoiding conflict, don't. Seek allies but don't abdicate your position. Understand the pitfalls of not engaging and balance them against the potential for reward. Engaging may be uncomfortable and threatening. You may find you raise some ire by standing up for your ideas. You may find yourself on the losing side, but managed properly, you will have gained in reputation and credibility. It may take courage the first few times, but you will soon see that if you are deliberate, dispassionate and direct, you will reap the remarkable rewards of respect and regard. If you are willing to engage but seek consensus, you may find yourself in a strong position. Defend your standpoint but demonstrate a willingness to listen to others and approach conflict collaboratively. You will be more likely to keep disagreement from turning negative. Having a reputation as someone who can be trusted to be open to others' angles on a topic can only result in building credibility capital.

Tolerating disagreement is not necessarily more positive than avoidance if the driver is power, political gain or a threat to them. Taking as their motto, the best defence is a good offence, these people focus on winning every battle and then the war. They are likely to willingly up the stakes from disagreement to conflict, figuring this is their playing field and they can outblock and tackle any opponent.

If you are the political player who seeks, perhaps seeds discord, stop! The payoffs are short-lived and the damage to your reputation sinks deep roots. It may be tempting to just overpower the opposition by dint of sheer force of personality, but don't. Over time your style will cost you. What you think is a sign of unwillingness to challenge you is actually the creation of an opposition that has gone underground. At some point you will need allies and when you look for them, no one will be there.

Those who are willing to address conflict tend to have strong communication skills. They are willing, perhaps eager, to debate details and perspectives. They can listen to their opposition and defend their point of view. Conversely, they are likely to be comfortable with a multiplicity of approaches and more willing to identify areas of agreement in disparate ideas.

SEPARATING THE CONTENT FROM THE PERSONAL

It can be easy to take disagreement personally. After all, they are taking issue with your perspective and point of view. This is where emotion turns disagreement into conflict and sends things south fast. It sounds simple enough to stay at the content level, but in truth it can be difficult to do.

Disagreement turns into conflict as the discussion leaves the realm of data and moves into that of emotion. Arguing for a certain perspective or plan includes an inherent notion that yours is the right one. One of the strongest emotions is that of certainty of your rightness. This is where the concept of face-saving surfaces. We tend to think that face-saving is the prime organizational directive. We do not want to be wrong and we certainly do not wish to be seen as weak. Not defending ourselves – that is, our position – means that we give up face. The Oxford Dictionary defines face-saving as 'the preserving of one's reputation, credibility, or dignity'. In a disagreement or conflict, this can mean defending ourselves and our rightness at the expense of the content and merits of the discussion itself. If we feel that our credibility capital will be diminished if we admit another's perspective is better than ours, we are certainly not going to give the proverbial inch.

As the emotions take over, we move from disagreement into conflict. We rely less on logic or data and more on assertions, assumptions and allegations. It is not unusual for the conversation to become personal: 'You were wrong last time and you are wrong this time.' 'Your approach always goes over budget.' 'You don't know what you're talking about. You weren't even here when we did this last time.' And as this goes on, the decibel level often rises as well. We are determined to win and this is no win-win situation. The goal has become win at all costs and take no prisoners.

It may feel that this is face-saving and building credibility, but it does not generally work that way. We may well shut down the discussion but that doesn't mean we gained converts. What we tend to gain is passive–aggressive opposition. We drive the discussion underground. People tend not to want to deal with unpleasantness, especially when it is directed at them. They retreat, but start to natter at our expense. The tone of the hall-talk would make our ears burn – if people didn't stop as soon as we rounded the corner.

Of course, not everyone will retreat. Your emotional response may move many to emotional responses in return. You know you are in the realm of emotions when examples and stories move from the discussion of today into the experiences of the past. Everyone has a virtual collection of gripe and grievance rocks. Sometimes, when we feel a particular rock is getting smaller and shrinking into forgetfulness, we will build it back up as we recall the specifics of our perceived ill-treatment or injury. We move it from past to present. This collection of grievances is particularly useful when discussion becomes personal. No one wins, but there is a perverse satisfaction in our righteous indignation over how we were wronged. So, rather than discuss today's issue's merits, we bring up stories of the past where our opponent – for by this point that is how matters have degraded – was wrong or unfair or behaved in some other real or perceived nefariousness manner. These stories are the rocks of our past injury and while they make us feel better, they serve no purpose, personal or professional.

The biggest issue with making disagreement personal is that it rarely remains in the conference room. Conflict between co-workers leads to lower productivity. We don't get as much done when focusing on our upset or anger. This in turn results in reduced job satisfaction. After all, daily contact with people with whom we have been trading barbs can be awkward at best and unpleasant and distressing at worst. There are always consequences to our actions. It is an unfortunate universal truth that negative actions have more impact on people than positive ones and will be remembered far longer.

So, if you want to maintain and build your credibility capital, keep your emotions in check. You will achieve more success if you can debate issues on their merits. Keep your emotions in check and your rocks out of the discussion. Remember, proving your rightness is not the goal, making the best decision for the organization is.

WILLINGNESS TO COMPROMISE

Part and parcel of keeping disagreement at the content level is a willingness to compromise. If you can give up your need to be right, it opens up a variety of options. In fact, it may be that there is a wholly new approach to the issue that belongs to none of the original parties. That's not to say that emotion is absent from compromise. It is not, but it takes on a much different patina than that of the emotions of conflict. Compromise requires respect. Respect for others and for the ideas of others. Respect does not mean deference. It means appreciating the validity of others' perspectives. It is built on trust and openness. Respect means actually listening to people without planning your response. Respect appreciates differences and the opportunities these provide to find creative, innovative and viable alternatives.

Respecting others is the first step towards compromise, but it is not the hardest step. That honour lies with a willingness to cede control. There is an irony here in that in truth no one really has control of events, of others' perceptions, of the structure of life. It is a hard lesson to learn and an even harder one to take to heart.

In organizations, this desire to control can become a hardened unwillingness to see possibility in different perspectives. That is the antithesis of respect. This means both a desire to dominate debate and discussion but also to regulate and restrict others' ability to participate. Compromise and respect in the organization means acknowledging the possibility of opportunity in perspectives other than our own.

The reason this feels so difficult and dangerous is that compromise can feel like surrendering and conceding the disagreement high ground. Moving from these emotions of control to a place of negotiation and conciliation requires effort. The all-too-human kneejerk reaction is to manoeuvre, manipulate and manage such that other ideas are quickly delegated to the dung heap. So, interrupting this automatic process takes conscious effort.

It also takes conscious effort to change how you perceive compromise. It is not loss. It is not injury to your reputation. It is not failure. It is a chance to create shared victory. Compromise requires vision and imagination. Compromise seeks a third or a fourth or a fifth path through the disagreement wilderness. Ironically, it is the inventiveness that comes out of compromise that moves the disagreement into new and positive territory. Once you open yourself to the possibility, even the probability that there is opportunity in different perspectives, the sky becomes the proverbial limit to what you and the organization can accomplish.

Disagreement is the natural order of human beings. We perceive events and issues differently and we become attached to the truth of our view of reality. Conflict does not have to be an inevitable result of disagreement. You have choice, make the right one.

CONFLICT TIPS FOR YOUR COMMUNICATION STYLE

How You Prepare Information	
Meticulous	*Holistic*
What Likely Works for You	What Likely Works for You
If you are meticulous, you are going to give a lot of thought to how you will present your thoughts and perspectives. When the discussion crosses the line to disagreement, this thoughtfulness can be of excellent value – if, when planning, you also thought about the opposition. Usually referred to as preemption, this involves actually developing the potential arguments and contrary perspectives. While this may seem counterintuitive, being able to think about what may come at you is an advantage and comes only from precision planning – your strong suit.	You are a natural strategic thinker. Keeping an eye on the big picture enables you to identify areas of agreement between differing perspectives that are invisible to others. You don't pay attention to the details but to the overall arc of the issue. Your ideas are at the 35,000-foot level, figuring the details can be sorted out later. You shine when the discussion gets into the weeds and you can bring it back to the bigger issues. This helps you maintain your credibility as it makes you seem less of a partisan and more of a facilitator. Done with authenticity and good humour, this can open space for opponents to see merit in both sides of an issue. An ability to think on your feet can enable you to react quickly when disagreement rears its unpleasant head.

What to Watch Out For	What to Watch Out For
There is a fine line between striving to be prepared and striving for perfection. The former is enabling, the latter can be, and often is, crippling. In the case of disagreement and conflict, this often shows up as a plan to have an answer to every single objection that could be raised, thereby stopping disagreement and conflict in their tracks. The thinking here is that if you have prepared perfectly, there can be no opposition. Sounds a bit ludicrous, doesn't it? Because you know perfectly well that there is always another idea or concept lurking around the corner that you did not think of when preparing. But, if you are super meticulous, that may mean you are not going to give up trying to find every single solitary potential objection in advance. All well and good, as long as you still pay attention to your side of the argument. So, sure, prepare. Give it your best thinking. Just know that someone or someones will have an objection of which you never had an inkling.	The downside of big picture thinking is that you may fail to pay attention to the specifics driving people's reactions. This can result in mis-analysing the core of the underlying issues driving people's strong emotional reactions. The devil really is in the details and while this may feel unnecessary to you, it matters deeply to others. Try first guiding the discussion to elicit the different perspectives, details and all before you move the conversation into broader perspectives. This will both endear your approach to others as well as build your credibility capital.

How You Convey Information

Direct	*Diplomatic*
What Likely Works for You	What Likely Works for You
If you are a highly direct person, you tend to be tolerant of disagreement primarily because you assume you can win it. Your communication style is clear and focused. This gives you an advantage over others who may have more difficulty marshalling their thoughts and rebuttals. If disagreement should devolve into conflict, your directness is likely to give you conflict acceptance as you are more than willing to engage when necessary. You see disagreement as a barrier to be surmounted and are comfortable in doing so.	Being diplomatic can mean that rather than tell people what to do, you are likely to ask them. Often, this can keep disagreement at bay because it opens up a space to discuss the issue calmly and openly. Not only are you careful in how you present your ideas, chances are you likely restate others' more combative statements into neutral terms. Your willingness to acknowledge that there can be more than one legitimate perspective and approach to an issue can lead people to focus on the final result rather than the specific way it is achieved. This, in turn, can help the group look for a pathway that encompasses more than one approach or idea.

What to Watch Out For	What to Watch Out For
While you tolerate disagreement, your focus is on the information at the expense of the people elements involved. You may inadvertently exacerbate the disagreement because you don't take time to address the personal perspectives and feelings involved. You are so focused on your points that you may – intentionally or not – begin to make the discussion personal and this can easily escalate disagreement to conflict. Your focus on the rightness of perspective can make compromise difficult, if not impossible.	The downside, however, of focusing on a multiplicity of approaches to a situation can make you too willing to cave, come disagreement time. Your tendency to speak carefully may be misinterpreted as a lack of commitment to your point of view. While this can keep conflict at bay, it will come at the cost of your credibility capital. All well and good to value diplomacy over direct confrontation. If, however, you are perceived as unwilling to advocate for your argument, your organization, or yourself, you will find yourself all too often on the losing side of the situation.

How You Receive Communication

Relational	*Substantive*
What Likely Works for You	What Likely Works for You
Empathetic people tend to be attentive to what others are saying and doing and why. This means when disagreement raises its often-contentious head, you will listen closely to what others are saying and, more importantly, why. Your focus may well be less on the specifics than on the perspective that spawned them. This allows you to identify the nascent personal elements that often lead to full-blown disagreement and subsequent conflict.	Your focus is on the substance of the communication, not the communicator. Fixated on goals and perspectives, your attention is laser-focused on the 'what' of the opposition rather than the 'why'. Your natural tendency is to listen to the arguments and the rationales that support them. This enables you to refute effectively and reinforce your position. You help keep the conversation on task or at the very least, keep the disagreement discussion on track by avoiding tangents and random examples.

What to Watch Out For	What to Watch Out For
Attentiveness to what others are saying and doing in a time of disagreement is all well and good, but not if it comes at the expense of being ready and able to promote your ideas and perspectives. Attentiveness can devolve into appeasement if your attention is solely on what others want and need. Being highly attentive means you tend to focus on others' input rather than your output. When the conversation gets tense, all of that focus on others can feel like sensory overload. In turn, that may lead you to retreat. Instead, listen for the key issues and perspectives and how they stack up against your point of view. You have your own kind of authority. Use it.	Focused on goals, you listen for support or opposition. When you pay attention to the words spoken but not the person speaking them, you can be perceived as being confrontive and dismissive. Worse, focused primarily on the content as it pertains to your side of the issue, everything else can feel extraneous and your behaviour may reflect that. People will notice and remember you did not demonstrate respect and that feeling of rejection has awfully long legs. So, pay attention.

How You Relate to Others

Collaborative	*Independent*
What Likely Works for You	What Likely Works for You
When disagreement raises its head, your first reaction is likely to try to pour oil on the troubled waters. You become facilitator as much, or more, than advocate, soliciting perspectives and trying to identify potential areas of agreement. It isn't that you lack a point of view, but that you are likely to see it as one of many perspectives that are valid approaches to the issue. You like working with others and see disagreement and conflict as something that can be resolved through consensus if everyone contributes and listens.	The proverbial individual contributor, focusing on your goals, you have a high tolerance for conflict because you rarely focus on feelings – your own or others. It is all about the ideas and approaches. It is easy for you to separate the content from the personal and you drive the dialogue in that direction. Your primary perspective is that the best approach should win the argument and you have spent hours researching, developing and honing yours.

What to Watch Out For	What to Watch Out For
Collaboration is all well and good, and often very desirable, but not at the expense of failing to support your own ideas and perspectives. If you spend your time during the discussion soliciting others' notions and approaches at the expense of advocating for your own, you are likely to see yours disappear, even if the result is more collaborative, thanks to your efforts. Make sure you stay true to yourself, even as you find ways to bring the group to consensus.	While you are not concerned about how people are feeling regarding the conflict and/or disagreement, rest assured others are. While they may appreciate the work you put into your ideas, they may also feel the same about their own. Your independence and willingness to engage and defend your interests in debate can make you look rigid, resulting in your opponents' own rigidity and unwavering support of their perspectives. This will not build your credibility capital and more likely, will diminish it. Try to engage with others' perspectives. It may not be comfortable at first, but it will earn you a lot of goodwill.

Your Communication Personality

Animated	*Controlled*
What Likely Works for You	What Likely Works for You
Your animated style is often engaging. You don't hold back when it comes to showing your feelings, so in times of disagreement or conflict, people do not have to guess where you stand. Your passion for your perspective is evident. Often, this style is persuasive and relatable and you may find that in the discussions on the issue, you make converts to your point of view.	You are engaged in the issues, but keep your feelings to yourself. Priding yourself on your objective, content-based approach, you do not think feelings have much to do with making organizational decisions. You can be the voice of reason when you analyse, compare and contrast the various perspectives during the discussion. Done well, you can lower the temperature of the argument and make room for real dialogue.
What to Watch Out For	What to Watch Out For
You may find yourself overpowering more reticent participants in the discussion. Your expressive style can easily become more forceful than persuasive. This can drive opposition underground, where people do not respond within the meeting but work behind your back to lobby against your position. Pay attention to how people are reacting. Notice if they have stopped responding. Take a breath. Ask questions to engage others. You may find leaving room for others to engage adds to your persuasiveness and credibility capital.	Your style is reserved. You pride yourself on being unexcitable, and while sometimes working in your favour, in times of disagreement and conflict you may well find yourself struggling for airtime. People can easily interpret your quieter style as a sign that you don't really care about the issue or lobbying for your side. In disagreement and conflict, this reticence can be deadly. You do not have to jump up and down and shout, but you do want to ensure people know you have a point of view.

12

Office Friends and Neighbours

We spend nearly three-quarters of our average week with a family of strangers with whom we must learn to live, co-operate, build, reflect and challenge. This randomly assigned family of co-workers will come from different upbringings, nationalities, educations, perspectives, values and beliefs yet it is from this group that we are expected to establish some of the most vital relationships in our lives. For that reason, it's understandable that we may come to think of them not merely as co-workers, but as friends. However important these relationships may be, it is important to be conscious that these are not friends in the most personal, conventional definition of the word and that professional boundaries must be maintained in the interest of your credibility.

We amass different kinds of friends at different points in our lives. Some stand the test of time, geography and personal growth, while others end up distant memories seen only in photos on our Facebook pages we keep on meaning to delete. That doesn't make us cold-hearted or unfeeling. No matter our intention to maintain relationships, friends come and go as our lives and situations change.

In the workplace, what we think of as friendship means something quite different, with its own distinct set of dynamics. These connections are inextricably tied to workplace exigencies, which add a layer of expectations not found in the personal social world. It becomes important, then, to be thoughtful about workplace friendships and relationships.

In a 2018 analysis of office friendships entitled *Friends Without Benefits*, Pillemer & Rothbard suggest that fundamentally the four pillars of friendship are: 'informality, voluntariness, communal norms and socioemotional goals'. These features, they argue, are in fundamental conflict with the four inherent qualities of relationships in organizations: 'formal roles, involuntary relationships, exchange norms and instrumental goals'.[1] Remember, the workplace is a socially artificial environment; the rules of engagement are based on a hierarchy, which in turn is based on a structure of boundaries. As Pillemer & Rothbard repeatedly note, personal friendship is rooted in choice and voluntary engagement. When it comes to the workplace, these elements of friendship are missing. At work, we are primarily focused on our job, our careers and making a living. While we may like and relate to some of our colleagues more than others, the free choices of relationships are greatly curtailed by a hierarchy and

---

[1]Pillemer, Julianna & Rothbard, Nancy P. (15 February 2018), 'Friends Without Benefits: Understanding the Dark Sides of Workplace Friendship', *Academy of Management Review* 43, No. 4: 635–60, https://doi.org/10.5465/amr.2016.0309

structure commanded by the work environment. In short, personal and professional relationships operate with a very different set of expectations, assumptions and structures. While not always mutually exclusive, these two frameworks do not always harmonize well.

One of the most consistently important components of a true friendship is the sharing of personal information. The workplace, however, is almost always the wrong place to be baring your soul and the 'informality and sharing of communal norms' that creates such rich friendships in personal life is fraught with peril in the workplace.[2] It is a slippery slope of self-revelation that will almost inevitably result in sharing too much. This can have a long-term effect on one's credibility by exposing potential vulnerabilities that can end up working against you when you least expect it.

This is not a semantic discussion of what constitutes friendship. Rather, it's a survival lesson in how not to lose sight of the dynamics of interpersonal relationships. These dynamics have an impact on what we expect from our colleagues and what they will expect from us in turn. Our credibility is impacted – for better or worse – by these interactions.[3]

We spend more time with our colleagues than we do with anyone else other than family, so thinking of them as friends makes some sense. Offering an important new take on mentoring, Kram & Isabella discuss the importance of what they called 'peer relationships' as an essential component of workplace emotional support.[4] Rawlins suggests that 'friends help in finding jobs and opportunities for promotion, provide support and third-party influence on important decisions and convey warnings about policy changes and "rumblings upstairs".'[5]

[2]Pillemer, Julianna & Rothbard, Nancy P. (15 February 2018), 'Friends Without Benefits: Understanding the Dark Sides of Workplace Friendship', *Academy of Management Review* 43, No. 4: 635–60, https://doi.org/10.5465/amr.2016.0309
[3]We are not taking a position on romantic relationships in the workplace. Those should be guided by specific company policies, made explicit by the organizations.
[4]Kram, Kathy E. & Isabella, Lynn A. (March 1985), 'Mentoring Alternatives: The Role of Peer Relationships in Career Development', *Academy of Management Journal* 28, No. 1: 110–32, https://doi.org/10.5465/256064
[5]Rawlins, Brad L. (1 April 2008), 'Measuring the Relationship between Organizational Transparency and Employee Trust', *Public Relations Journal* 2, No. 2, https://doaj.org

These work relationships are important. They help us navigate organizational political waters and understand norms and expectations. Human beings are at heart social creatures and in general, we are hard-wired to cultivate peer relationships. What this means is our default mode is to establish relationships for most of us and we think of at least some of these people as good friends. Generally, challenges to these instincts only arise when we touch the hot stove of ill-chosen sharing one too many times. Then, and often only then, do we learn the hard lesson. But if we know we have a predisposition to touch that stove, we can protect ourselves in advance by setting personal boundaries that allow us to keep these peer relationships in perspective to maintain our credibility. However, that's not as easy as it sounds.

It is easy to confuse a good working relationship with friendship, especially when working with people with whom you share an enthusiasm to succeed. Teams thrive when members become closer and more engaged. Additionally, they often produce a more substantial work product. More and more companies today utilize some sort of team approach to solutions and getting the work done. This almost inevitably propels the leap from peer to friend.

There are a multitude of studies supporting the importance of teams for organizational effectiveness and business success. Teams stimulate an exchange of ideas, breed trust and develop camaraderie, producing results that are more than the sum of the participant parts. Organizations, private, public and non-profit, have learned this lesson and it has become a kind of management touchstone so it makes sense that organizations of all stripes would encourage work relationships-friendships. Building these bonds, however, can come at a price. Pillemer & Rothbard suggest that while 'mutual self-disclosure and perceived similarity between colleagues encourage the development of friendship and its associated benefits'[6] they can also lead to oversharing that impacts achieving the very results teams were designed to create.

[6]Pillemer, Julianna & Rothbard, Nancy P. (15 February 2018), 'Friends Without Benefits: Understanding the Dark Sides of Workplace Friendship', *Academy of Management Review* 43, No. 4: 635–60, https://doi.org/10.5465/amr.2016.0309

In the free-flowing, free-spending 1980s Steven was the PR representative for a TV station in a major media market. Competition in this market among stations was intense, never more so than during the traditional February and November ratings periods. These months, often referred to as 'sweeps', were part of a Nielsen (and at the time Arbitron) ratings system of measurement that allowed for the setting of ad rates for the remainder of the year. In this market, the competition was especially brutal for local news and video feature magazine programming. Millions were spent on elaborate stunts, travel and advertising to get a coveted sweeps ratings victory. All of this involved thousands of hours of work from teams of reporters, producers and editors, who pretty much gave up their personal lives for weeks at a time to win this TV war twice a year. At the end of each sweeps period there was always a highly anticipated and much-hyped blow-out party to celebrate the hopeful victory. Winning was everything. What made these parties unique, however, was they had a no spouse, no significant other invitation policy. A no-tell 'cone of silence' was imposed on these events. Alcohol was always served in abundance that often resulted in dancing on tables and couples disappearing throughout the night in drunken hazes. It was management's calculated decision that these opportunities to blow off some steam and foster intradepartmental relationships would manifest in a comradery that would result in harder work among the staff. The permission to allow in 'outsiders' would distract from that level of commitment. While such practices would give HR a collective coronary today, that formula at the time undeniably worked. Year after year, people worked tirelessly and the station maintained an unmatched string of ratings wins. As for the interpersonal relationships such a practice encouraged? It was the eighties! There was no tracking of harassment charges, marriage and/or divorces at these pre-meditated social/work gatherings, just the continuous planning for the next exclusive bonding party.

MISCONSTRUED PAIRINGS

It's ironic that so many recruiters use the draw of an open, friendly workplace that rewards relationships and teamwork without suggesting guidelines for those relationships. Fortunately, HR often steps in during the on-boarding process to provide policy guardrails. HR has the task of preserving vital decorum at work and protecting individuals and the organization. When managed thoughtfully, HR's guidance is the key to maintaining a healthy and safe environment in which everyone can succeed. It's ironic that so many recruiters use the draw of an open, friendly workplace that rewards relationships and teamwork without suggesting guidelines for those relationships.

Today, there is a justifiable heightened awareness of everyone's personal relationships at work, resulting in an even greater need to closely monitor workplace relationships. There is a laser focus on fairness, diversity and opportunity intended to correct generations of often ignored practices. Lines crossed today are swiftly called out and punished. So, the question remains, how do you create constructive bonds with co-workers that preserve an individual's credibility and have the desired effect that fosters that growth and upward mobility? It's a delicate dance that ultimately comes down to personal responsibility and an environment that rewards a high level of respect among its workers.

FAMILIARITY AND MISUNDERSTANDING

Communication is both the cause and casualty of office relationship-friendships. It's far too easy to assume familiarity enables fast and accurate understanding. Sometimes people or teams develop a kind of shorthand. This may work well within the team, but it may be distancing and confusing to others. Besides, even within the team, emotion and feelings can colour understanding such that misinterpretation results. The assumption of understanding among familiar co-workers can often result in huge gaps in knowledge that can create a snowball of misunderstanding.

Cliques are a natural outgrowth of this level of group intimacy and can take on their own personality as perceived by outsiders. Cliques are of use only to those in them. Overall, they can create an us-versus-them mentality that serves no one. Nowhere is the damage to credibility and communication seen more than where there are disagreements between co-workers within and without of these complicated cliquish relationships. Like most conflicts, as we explained in Chapter 8, Non-Verbal Communication (*see also* pp. 96–111), the unspoken interests of parties in conflict can get in the way of arbitrating and negotiating disagreements. Add in a layer of complicated interpersonal relationships and you have a hornet's nest of emotion that may make the conflict unmanageable as well as indecipherable.

Even when there is a tight group bond, it behoves everyone to remember that there is more at stake than the relationships of the individuals. In the organization, the results to be produced become an overlay on any workplace relationship. This overlay is the principal difference between social and workplace friendships.

It's important to remember that your boss is not your friend. You may have an encounter at a party or networking event where it feels like the two of you are on an equal footing. You may even have found a topic of shared interest, such as your kids' football leagues or a mutual love of Miniature Schnauzers or sport fishing. Do not misinterpret that collegial conversation for a bridge to establishing a friendship. Furthermore, revealing more about yourself in that artificially social environment will not help you towards your next promotion. In fact, it is much more likely to be career limiting. Know the boundaries. Your bosses certainly do.

Staying vigilant and keeping perspective in outside-of-work social situations is not reserved for communication with your boss. It's much trickier in one of those informal gatherings to maintain those boundaries in dialogue with co-workers. This can be lunch, or it might be one of those group social activities. Never forget almost every interaction that involves the imbibing of alcohol has within it the possibility of near or long-term disaster. The permanency of a digital photo taken at an inopportune time might even have a greater impact than an offhand comment. As we've learned about the varying levels of formality between phone, email, posting and texting, communication with peers in a friendly environment can easily take on an easily misconstrued tone at best and career threatening at worst. It's those blurred lines that gets us in the most trouble and the casual gathering is a breeding ground for confusing intentions and credibility killers.

For social networking in particular, be very careful. If it's just too irresistible to post last night's pasta primavera or your wet dog running through the kitchen, then establish multiple accounts for your work friends and other friends. Not that this ever gives you an excuse to be reckless, but it does allow you to compartmentalize your life. The beauty of LinkedIn is that its very tendency to be stuffy and overly business-like makes it a site for serious business postings. With a zero-fun environment, there is little motivation to clutter your postings with frivolous off-topic messaging. Social networking sites like Facebook and Twitter have made it intentionally confusing as their own business models have evolved. What started as fun and games and new ways to connect has given way to cultivating new revenue sources that look to encourage business communication and transactions on their sites. For that reason, the lines you draw are vitally important when messaging and posting for co-workers.

All of this discussion is designed not to make you fearful of everything you do, just to make you aware that there are almost always consequences to your actions. It's about responsibility. Responsibility to yourself to preserve your credibility and to your co-workers to not always act on your impulses. So, what is the trick to office friendships? There is no trick because 99 per cent of the time office friendships aren't friendships at all. They are peer relations driven by situational encounters that may last for years, but should not be thought of as much more than circumstantial. There is nothing wrong with cordial and lively relations with co-workers as long as you keep a close eye on the boundaries. A true test of your friendship will not emerge while you share the same employer, but rather after you have gone your separate 'business ways'. If the relationship transcends that, then you have made yourself a real friend in the truest sense of the word.

WORK RELATIONSHIP TIPS FOR YOUR
COMMUNICATION STYLE

How You Prepare Information	
Meticulous	*Holistic*
What Likely Works for You	What Likely Works for You
Your penchant for preparation likely means you rarely take communication for granted. You are going to think about what you say, including in more social conversations. You do not want to be misunderstood or your intentions questioned. When you make a request, you have figured out what you want to say, where you want to say it and to whom. While this will give you comfort and confidence, it may make you seem something less than authentic. So, make sure you smile.	When you are part of any social planning, your penchant to brainstorm is apt to be a great asset. 'What if we …' statements share your thoughts and can trigger others to think a bit more creatively. Be careful, however, that you stay focused on your organization and your colleagues. Ideas that may work well for 'friend' friends can be disastrous for work friends.
What to Watch Out For	What to Watch Out For
If you find yourself in an uncomfortable situation, make sure you make your thoughts known immediately. Whether being pressured to contribute to a colleague's birthday gift or join the basketball pool or socialize outside of the office, do not try to plan the perfect phrasing. Sometimes spontaneity is the way to go.	Thinking aloud can mean that musings become plans and you become the planner. So, be wary of just wondering because people may interpret the idea as a blueprint. Your inclination to dive in with ideas may put you in awkward situations if you just happen to join a conversation. Sometimes you need to think about the implications and potential complications of your words. If you find yourself in that uneasy place, just lightly let people know they are welcome to your ideas and walk away. An idea is not a commitment to participate.

How You Convey Information	
Direct	*Diplomatic*
What Likely Works for You	What Likely Works for You
Your straightforward approach to communication will leave no doubt about your thoughts on pretty much any issue, work or social. If you do not want to participate in an out-of-the-office social event, you will make your intentions clear. If you do, people will know that, too.	Concerned as you are as to how people will react to your words, you want to be sure there is no misunderstanding around your motivations. This is true especially if you don't wish to participate in a company social activity. When you organize an activity, you will make sure people feel they have a choice. No forced camaraderie from you.
What to Watch Out For	What to Watch Out For
Your candidness can create issues if you are not careful and observant. If you turn down an invitation bluntly, people may interpret this as a complete rejection of them as well as of the event. You don't want to inadvertently throw away the workplace relationships needed to get things done just because you do not wish to socialize at a Friday night happy hour. If you are the organizer, however, you just might be so assertive as to leave people feeling they have no choice but to join in. When people feel forced, there is almost always a bad outcome, so rein it in.	Make sure you do not put concern for people's potential reactions to your words ahead of what you really want to do. Otherwise, you are likely to discover yourself involved with planning the holiday party when you really did not even want to go. You can be gracious, but make sure you make your wants and needs known.

How You Receive Communication	
Relational	*Substantive*
What Likely Works for You	What Likely Works for You
You pay such close attention to others' perceptions and perspectives, it is apt to be easy for you to figure out what may be going on behind the rhetorical scenes. As the work friend world is embedded in the work political universe, it makes sense to look for ulterior motives. Sometimes an invitation to an after-work social hour is just that and nothing more. If you listen well, as is your wont, you will be able to tell if there is some intelligence gathering intention involved.	You focus on the 'what' rather than the 'who' of communication. In the work-friends realm this can mean you identify early where there is a push for something in which you are not interested. This enables you to let others know what you are interested in participating in and what you are not.
What to Watch Out For	What to Watch Out For
Paying attention to others' wants and needs is a good quality, but not if it comes at the expense of yours.	While you focus on the content signals, you tend to dismiss, and sometimes flat out ignore, the people signals regarding their intentions and perspectives. As counterintuitive as it might seem, understanding these can help make it easier to refuse involvement in activities that just don't suit your fancy.
How You Relate to Others	
Collaborative	*Independent*
What Likely Works for You	What Likely Works for You
You build relationships which likely means that people are interested in including you in their activities. You are apt to take on their interests as your own, however, so don't let your natural warmth be misinterpreted. Identify early on the pursuits that appeal to you and endeavour to stay true to those.	People will learn early on where your work friends' boundaries are because you make that truly clear. Not averse to conflict, you probably are not worried about the potential fallout from a social activity ignored. If they want to debate it, you are willing to accommodate them.

What to Watch Out For	What to Watch Out For
Your friendliness is likely seen as friendship with all the rights and responsibilities thereto. If you don't watch out, you may fall into a pattern of developing work friends who see themselves as 'friend' friends. This can put you into a role which sometimes, people pleaser that you are, you find it difficult from which to extricate yourself. So, be willing to say no. Nicely, but no.	There are social elements in the workplace that ignoring may put you at a disadvantage. Cultivating some work friends will give you allies and you may find that useful down the road. So, if accepting some social invitations helps you gain those useful relationships, just do it. Who knows? You might even find them fun.

Your Communication Personality

Animated	*Controlled*
What Likely Works for You	What Likely Works for You
You may well be the proverbial life and soul of the party so if there is a work social event, people will want and expect you to join in. This will definitely up your popularity quotient. While you may not always feel like joining, you are apt to feel you ought to anyway.	You have the advantage of a reserved demeanour which enables you to decide what and when you want to engage in the work social niceties. This can help you avoid those situations in which you are either uncomfortable or uninterested. Just don't let your reticence get out of hand – people and relationships can be valuable in building your career.
What to Watch Out For	What to Watch Out For
Your expressive style can be misinterpreted as enthusiasm, however. You may find yourself planning a social event you never even wanted to attend because you could not help your animated self. Make sure when you are really enthusiastic, they know. And when you are not, they know that as well.	If you are too hard to read, keeping your cards and feelings close to your chest, people may begin to give up on any kind of friendship. This is because what you may feel is just being true to yourself, they see as rejection. People hate to be rebuffed and they will protect themselves by ignoring you. That puts you, not them, at a disadvantage. So, say yes occasionally – it won't hurt at all!

13

6 to an 8

Why do we sometimes want to be something we're not? Often it is because of success projection. Success projection means emulating those we believe have all the traits of a leader. Becoming as passionate as Steve Jobs, as persuasive as Tony Robbins, or as inspiring as Martin Luther King are great goals, but it misses the point of the individual power of those people. Mimicking others is inauthentic and counterproductive so rather than try to mould yourself into something entirely new, better to figure out how to make the most of your inherent style and strengths.

Authenticity is inherently persuasive, so the more your communication is true to you, the more people are likely to respond to it. That doesn't mean you can just write off any and all challenges or slip ups in the name of authenticity. What it does mean is that you can and should strategically assess and target your own individual strengths and weaknesses as a communicator to maximize the impact of your personal voice.

Many people hate the notion of a numbered scale for the basis of personal performance, but grading and measuring does give us some structure for gauging improvement. In reality, numerical rankings are so subjective as to be almost useless. Ranking implies a standardized, one-size-fits-all approach to effective communication that can be often found in online recommendations, most self-help books and costly seminars. It implies everyone with enough work can become a Jobs or an Obama or a Churchill or a King. It's a false promise. Besides, rankings don't really get to the heart of the matter. What should be evaluated is how you are perceived as a presenter and overall communicator. In personal presentation training, we look to establish a baseline of performance – a start from which we can build. Then you can strengthen your skills for specific communications contexts and goals.

Most people already have a decent sense of how effective they are as communicators and look for that level of honesty from professionals beyond the coddling from friends, family and subordinates. They usually want us to tell them how we would rate them on that cold scale of 1–10. Then, they figure, we can tell them what to do to reach that 'perfect' 10 rating. For better or worse, improving public speaking skills doesn't quite work that way. There is no universal scale of excellence, but there is a personal scale of excellence – and that is authenticity. We all have images of those who we believe to be level 10 speakers. We admire their ability to connect with an audience and want to achieve that ourselves. Mimicking them is not the answer – even if we could do it. What is important is to understand what makes us authentic speakers and then learn how we can improve our skills and raise our personal best to a 6 or an 8 and then to a 10, all while remaining true to our authentic selves.

Also, as we keep reminding you in this book, communication never takes place in a vacuum. What counts as effective communication in one context may be a flop in another. With that in mind, your goal should be to understand what you bring to every communication event. You are a total package. A collection of attributes that are the raw materials for presentations and the ability to present yourself convincingly and credibly. That means embracing your inherent strengths and addressing your shortcomings.

Some people are just shy by nature and the act of delivering a presentation or talk is as terrifying as the thought of open-heart surgery. Others are okay in a small group, but are subject to panic and brain freeze in a gathering larger than three or four. And others love being the centre of attention, are good at telling stories and confident in their ability to command a room, never lacking for something to say. We call that last group *The Three Percenters*, a term we unscientifically derived. Most people are in the 97 per cent of the population who find speaking before any size group challenging at best, debilitating at worst. Whichever category you're in, the good news is that when you harness your intrinsic strengths, there is a natural niche you can cultivate for yourself.

If you are generally a little introverted, take heart. You possess a quality shared by 30 per cent of the population according to Susan Cain's book *Quiet: The Power of Introverts in a World That Can't Stop Talking*, which embraced the values of being a thoughtful and, oftentimes, a shy person.[1] The benefit of being a genuine introvert is that it gives you a relatable quality which can actually help you connect with an audience. Relatability equals likeability and that allows you to connect with your listeners.

You want to remember that people aren't listening to evaluate how well you do against some mythical classic rules of successful public speaking. They are listening to what you have to say because of what

---

[1]Cain, Susan (2013), *Quiet: The Power of Introverts in a World That Can't Stop Talking*, New York: Broadway Books.

you have accomplished, what you know, what you do. In short, it is your credibility capital that makes what you are saying meaningful to your audience.

The credibility capital you bring to any talk will have a powerful influence on how you are perceived as a communicator. Here, the lesson is not to diminish the basics of good content planning and sound performance techniques, it's just to point out that there are always other factors at play which can influence what is perceived to be effective communication. There is a reason you are the presenter. You may not be famous, but you have experience, knowledge, facts and a point of view to share. Stay connected to that and you will do fine.

When it comes to communicating and presenting, some people think that the higher they move up the ranks, the more important it is to be the mythical level 10 speaker. This is the greatest trap into which you can fall. The skills that got you there will be the skills that will make you successful in that new role.

At one point Steven had an opportunity presented to raise the communicator score of an executive to maximize his chances of being considered for the CEO position of a major media conglomerate. At the time, the company was looking to fill a position in a new studio structure and had set up an unusual very public competition, or what some began to call a corporate 'bake-off'. There were three high-level executives within the company who would be part of this challenge for the top post. The executive VP of Worldwide Marketing was putting her chips on the current studio president, with whom she had the closest relationship, and probably saw him as the best way to safeguard her own position. She wanted us to raise his game to make him a true contender, but this had to be done in a clandestine way because it was clearly stated by the company chairman that there were to be no intentional transformations or campaigning for the position.

The general assumption was that in the presentation-focused entertainment business when an executive rose to a certain level business, they had to demonstrate a very animated and gregarious style. This particular executive didn't naturally thrive in the kind of internal and external podium-style presentations that would be essential should he rise to this top position. He was, however, a phenomenally creative executive and former literary agent with deep relationships with some of the studio's most gifted producers and directors, among them Christopher Nolan, Guillermo del Toro, Tim Burton and Ben Affleck. His more softly-spoken, thoughtful personality was a great match for producers, writers and directors, with whom he gave confidence that they would be protected and nurtured within the studio system. Reading scripts, giving notes and cultivating relationships with talented performers was the part of the job that he found most rewarding and which made him one of the most respected studio heads.

What Steven stressed to this executive was that people want to listen to, and be led by, someone who is enthusiastic and cares about what they do, because they want to find the same feeling in themselves. It's that believable quality that allows you to build on your relationship with any size audience and lets you share your personal vision in any industry. The more often you can share that emotion, the less you will need to rely on notes when you present, and you'll be more apt to convince an audience that you mean what you say and you're worth listening to. It isn't about how you share that enthusiasm, it is that you let it show through.

This client worked tirelessly to improve his skills and confidence and become more accepting of what he was versus what others thought he should be. He learned the power of focusing on telling stories about the successes in his career that brought him the greatest satisfaction as a creative executive. In the end he didn't get the job, but his hard work on his communication did pay off: he became the head of his own studio and a producer of films in which he deeply believed. No question, he achieved his own level of '10' as the result of the coaching that helped him better communicate who he was as an executive and as a person.

Focusing on what fuels you, what fills your life with enthusiasm and passion will make a talk more compelling. Cultivating and remembering our connection to the topic at hand, why it is important and why we care about it is the key to allowing us to be better messengers and to build-out our credibility capital. Inevitably, though, you have to speak about something that doesn't ignite you. You may have to present someone else's ideas or do one more repeat of a pitch or a sales presentation. That's the nature of life. The good news is that there are some valuable ways to go about the process that allow you to get a better sense of who you are, how you can be the most effective and more consistently tap into your credibility capital.

Start out by thinking of the moments in your life when you feel you have been the most successful at communicating your message. That goes for your personal as well as work life. And by successful, we don't just mean in the room at the time, but also in the aftermath where you feel that your message made a lasting impact. Think of the circumstances. Was it because it was a subject you knew the most about? Was it because you had a willing audience? Was it set up positively by others? Or maybe it was when you were forced to deliver bad news and you could provide perspective that helped a group take your messaging to heart? In any of these cases, identifying the underlying source of your effectiveness will allow you to use that as a framework for how you can be more impactful every time you speak.

Some of this goes against human nature. We tend to look at what didn't work rather than what did. It's that dwelling on the negative that keeps us stuck in the past rather than creating a positive vision of our speaking prowess in the future. Focus on what you did well and create a vision of yourself as a successful speaker. Of course, your mental state is only half the game. The other half consists of specific practices that will allow you to fine-tune your messaging in subtle but impactful ways.

You can think of a presentation as a kind of monologue, an opportunity to give others a glimpse of what drives you. You want to focus on the reason for your talk. Why are you there? Work backwards. Never lose sight of your concluding message. Sometimes you will want to tell them the end first. When the news is bad, the rule of thumb is never bury the headline. Be direct. Be open. You will have done a disservice to yourself and to the audience if you make them jump through linguistic rings of fire.

People dread being the bearer of bad news. There is often a drive to make rhetorical lemonade out of the lemon of a message. Never a good idea to try to sell the unsaleable. People know when someone is trying to put lipstick on the pig of bad news. They feel demeaned because it means the speaker doesn't think they are smart enough to read between the lines. But they are and they do. So, sometimes the best you can get from them is 'Well, at least they aren't lying to us.'

As a presenter, Jane was a self-critical '6' and wanted this particular speech, which she saw as one of the most important of her career, to be a '10'. She had bad news to convey and was so concerned about delivering it to her team that she went out and hired someone to write this difficult speech for her. The result was a thoughtful and literate script, but it was also a long and winding road of disconnected analogies and not so subtle references to the dark cloud's silver lining. More importantly, the speech was not a reflection of who she was as a leader and as a person.

Jane practiced the purchased prose for weeks and in the end delivered it well, hardly looking at the pages on her lectern. The speech was well done. Unfortunately, as she held smaller sessions for more in-depth discussion on the news, her communication floundered. Jane quickly discovered that the words in the speech were at odds with her own personal, relatable thoughts and reflections on the topic. Trying to stay within the confines of those created analogies hurt her authenticity and ultimate effectiveness. She went for the '10' in the moment, but in the classic sense, won the battle and lost the communication war. Her credibility took a major hit among her team members as they viewed her actions as inauthentic and false. Jane's intentions were good, but her process was flawed and she paid the price of self-betrayal.

Always remember the mission is to deliver an authentic, lasting, meaningful message that represents you as an individual. So, dispense with the numbers. Spend more time thinking about you and what you bring to the public speaking table. Embrace who you are as a person, warts and all. Always practise the process of telling your story in the most meaningful and easily understandable way. If you do that, you will achieve your own kind of credibility capital that is literally off the charts.

PRESENTATION TIPS FOR YOUR COMMUNICATION STYLE

How You Prepare Information	
Meticulous	*Holistic*
What Likely Works for You	What Likely Works for You
You think plan, organize and prepare ahead. This enables you to maximize your strengths in advance. You go into the talk secure in the knowledge that you have given yourself every edge possible.	You are ready to move away from your original approach if the situation calls for it. This flexibility can give you the insight needed to connect with your audience. As you do it from your inherent approach to communication, it has the advantage of being part of your core authenticity.
What to Watch Out For	What to Watch Out For
Planning does not mean perfecting. Audiences and talks have a way of going their own way, so be prepared for detours along your planned route.	You are somewhat impatient when it comes to preparing your talk. You get a few ideas in your head and you are ready to rock and roll. Much of the time this is all you have to do to be effective – much but not all. Be willing to prepare and plan when the consequences of failure are significant.
How You Convey Information	
Direct	*Diplomatic*
What Likely Works for You	What Likely Works for You
Your directness will be helpful in making sure you are staying connected to your authentic self. You think about your information and how to communicate it straightforwardly and precisely. That said, match your style to the situation. A little versatility never hurts.	You pay attention to how people are reacting to what you have to say. This insight into how well you are connecting with your listeners gives your talk a strong authenticity because it is so much of who you are.

What to Watch Out For	What to Watch Out For
Your focus on information is all well and good, but you are not connecting to information. You are connecting to people. Keep that in mind.	Content is still king, however, so don't give it short shrift. As you build your talk, think about how people will receive it. You can maximize how they respond to your message by thinking about it in advance.

How You Receive Communication

Relational	*Substantive*
What Likely Works for You	What Likely Works for You
When you think about your talk you are apt to think of it from audience forward. This enables you to focus on their perceptions and what those mean for your ability to achieve your goals.	Your attention is on what you want to say and how to defend your position. You do this cerebrally, logically and with as much rationality as you can muster. You listen to your audience the same way. This enables you to stay focused on your goals for the talk.
What to Watch Out For	What to Watch Out For
Don't let their perceptions drive you too far off your chosen road. Use them to help guide your talk so you achieve your purpose. Remember, you are the one making the pitch and you have something you want and need to accomplish. Add that to your focus, too.	Always remember that people have a less than rational component to their thinking. Whether you see it as emotion or sentiment, excitement, or passion, these very human feelings have a role in persuasion. They work in conjunction with the more logical elements in determining how people will react. Ignore them at your peril.

How You Relate to Others

Collaborative	*Independent*
What Likely Works for You	What Likely Works for You
You are apt to expect that your open-hearted sincerity and concern for others will be the deciding factor in your audience's engagement with you and your talk. Much of the time you are right and reap the rewards and benefits.	You are comfortable standing up for yourself and your point of view. Your authenticity is bound up in your willingness to advocate even in the face of resistance and opposition. People expect this of you and respect it.

What to Watch Out For	What to Watch Out For
People may react well to your authentic self but that may not transfer to your ideas and arguments. Make sure you give the same attention to how they are reacting to the points of your talk as you do to their reactions to you personally. You are going to need both to succeed.	Be a bit wary of focusing so much on your points that you forget that people have their own ideas that might be different. You can try to out-argue and debate them, but that may not achieve the results you desire. Be careful not to browbeat. People may stop arguing but that does not mean they have changed their perspective.

Your Communication Personality

Animated	*Controlled*
What Likely Works for You	What Likely Works for You
You are easy to read and people often interpret that as authentic. Your communication is usually expressive, often vivid and occasionally a bit flamboyant. As long as this matches the situation, you may well be in the communication power seat.	Measured and disciplined in your presentation style, you are not an emotive speaker. Rather, you are reserved and prefer to let your material be your persuasive entrée to the presentation. This moderate approach can give your talk that important air of authenticity.
What to Watch Out For	What to Watch Out For
Make sure your style matches the situation. Connecting with a large audience requires more powerful presence than in a small group. Rein it in when the physicality of the situation demands it.	Just make sure that you bring some energy into your talk along with your good arguments. Remember the impact stories can have and try hard to incorporate them. A little bit of narrative woven around your arguments can go a long way towards connecting with your audience.

14

Zooming In

Widely used video chatting, presenting and communicating is here to stay, whether we like it or not. Practically the minute telephonic communication became common, people began dreaming of actually seeing the person on the other end of the wire. It took decades after the PicturePhone was presented by Bell Systems at their 1964 New

York World's Fair pavilion, for internet technology to enable this novelty to become a reality. Whether it's FaceTime, Teams, Webex, Zoom, Skype or whatever the video application flavour of the moment, today's smartphones, laptops and iPads interconnect with high-definition cameras in an instant. Whereas plain old telephones only required controlling and worrying about your voice, and few even paid attention to that, video means having to think about your facial expressions, body movement, clothing, surroundings and all the visual factors that communicate to the person who you are and what you have to say. If that doesn't sound daunting, you aren't paying close enough attention. It is a whole new way of thinking about physical context. As we pointed out in Chapter 4 Perception is Reality (*see also* pp. 50–58), people interpret everything about you – even when they do not realize they are doing so. It is all about managing those perceptions and the more variables in play, the more elements there are to manage.

For the moment, video chatting is the ultimate cool medium. In this context, 'cool' does not refer to popular or relevant. The concept of cool media comes from a concept media theorist Marshall McLuhan, who described movies in his 1964 book, *Understanding Media: The Extensions of Man*,[1] as a 'hot media' because cinema visually immerses and surrounds us so requires little active participation to feel involved in the experience. He classified television, at least as it was in the 1960s, as the ultimate cool media because it offered a less complete and stimulating experience which required the viewer to be more actively involved with bringing meaning to what they were seeing. Today's television experience is no longer a cool medium. High Definition (HD), extra-large screens, immersive production values and surround sound systems clearly meet McLuhan's criteria for a hot media. Communication through Zoom-type connectivity returns us to that cool medium McLuhan referred to, as at this point in development, it only offers a relatively passive, non-involving experience.

[1]McLuhan, Marshall (1994), *Understanding Media: The Extensions of Man*, 1st MIT Press ed., Cambridge, Mass: MIT Press.

More recent research focuses on the concept of media richness.[2] Media richness expands on McLuhan's notions by looking at how much information can be conveyed by a medium. A richer medium such as face to face can communicate more information more quickly than a leaner medium such as written communication. Video communication is richer than an email or a phone call, but not so rich as face to face. Understanding the four components of media richness can help you make your use of video more effective. These are: 1) access to multiple cues, 2) immediacy of feedback, 3) variety in the use of language and images, and 4) being able to personalize your communication to your audience.

Video allows you to use more non-verbal cues than a phone call. Your facial expression is the most obvious additive cue as it indicates both emotion and interest. Gestures, eye contact – albeit with the camera – responding to others' cues all work to make video a richer medium. The camera allows for more immediate feedback as well. You can and should watch your audience. Note their expressions and their eye contact. You can tell a lot from this and use this feedback to guide you, taking advantage of this element of media richness. Video allows you to use a variety of communication cues to reach your audience. You have access to more than words, thanks to the ability to share your screen. Numbers, charts, graphs and photos are the kind of rich visual aids that add to the amount of information shared. Lastly, video allows personalization to the audience. You can determine how to adapt your communication and your information to the audience in real time. Taking advantage of the potential for rich communication via video will make you more effective and ultimately, more credible.

Video, for all its advantages, is still a medium fraught with peril. It leaves plenty of room for minds and attention to wander. In short, whether you look at the video communication medium from the perspective as potentially rich or inherently cool, it's harder to be good and next to impossible to be great without preparation, analysis and self-awareness.

[2]Daft, Richard L. & Lengel, Robert H. (May 1986), 'Organizational Information Requirements, Media Richness and Structural Design', *Management Science* 32, No. 5: 554–71, https://doi.org/10.1287/mnsc.32.5.554

The rapid and broad acceptance of seeing someone you're talking to virtually was the result of the high cost of travel as well as the surge in working from home, which was exacerbated by the COVID-19 pandemic. There is no doubt that COVID-19 served as the fast forward button for expansion of video calling. Even before that, however, as technology improved, organizations were encouraging increased use of virtual meetings. The numbers are staggering. Remote working grew 159 per cent between 2005 and 2017.[3] By 2020, an estimated 58 per cent of businesses reported using video conferencing as part of their daily way of doing business. Three-quarters of CEOs forecast that video conferencing will soon replace the oft-dreaded conference call. It is a big business and growing. Clearly, being able to use this medium well is critical to building credibility capital.

The future is clear: virtual meetings are not going away. No doubt technology will continue to improve the experience, you will always have to achieve success in virtual communication differently than in-person. And, of course, there is always the personal reaction to having to see yourself on video: 'I don't like the way I look!' Filho, Inkpen & Czerwinski found that 'users seemed to favor filters that make subtle changes to their appearance, or, in some instances, they preferred to use an avatar instead'.[4] Vanity does not disappear when we are in front of the camera – it increases!

Over the years, both of us have provided media training for hundreds of executives and personalities in a variety of industries. Rule of thumb for this kind of coaching is taping the person in mock interview sessions. It is the best way to understand what works and what doesn't. We have learned that most of the time our participants would rather be at the dentist! We estimate fewer than 2 per cent ever ask to see or hear their recordings. Sometimes we insist, but usually we don't. If seeing yourself is going to make you overly self-conscious

[3]Flexjobs (2017), 'The 2017 State of Telecommuting in the U.S. Employee Workforce Report', https://www.flexjobs.com/2017-State-of-Telecommuting-US
[4]Filho, Jose Eurico de Vasconcelos, Inkpen, Kori M. & Czerwinski, Mary (2009), 'Image, Appearance and Vanity in the Use of Media Spaces and Video Conference Systems', in *Proceedings of the ACM 2009 International Conference on Supporting Group Work – GROUP '09* (Proceedings of the ACM 2009 international conference, Sanibel Island, Florida), USA: ACM Press, 253, https://doi.org/10.1145/1531674.1531712

and take your focus off the event and onto yourself, perhaps a little ignorance is bliss.

Some of this may be generational. Gen X and Gen Z are a lot more accustomed to seeing and hearing themselves on video than are Baby Boomers. From infancy, they were photographed and videoed intensely, due to improved immediate technologies. They were soon on Instagram, Snapchat, YouTube and Facebook. They know how they look and are far more comfortable with video as a result of those experiences. However, they may still choose to turn off the video in a business setting if they are feeling they aren't camera ready or are not implored to keep it on. They may be comfortable on camera, but they have learned how to burnish and protect their image!

Think about how to take advantage of the potential in video and maximize the opportunity of it as a rich medium. In 1967, noted researcher Albert Mehrabian conducted two independent studies on non-verbal communications and the findings were that body language and tone of voice can make up a staggering 93 per cent of how we communicate.[5] Just because you are not on video does not mean that the importance of non-verbal communication diminishes. In fact, as we discussed earlier in our chapter about Context, it becomes more important.

The potential benefits of today's video communications are obvious. The limitations are as well. It may be immediate, but it is still virtual. It's an opportunity for you make a visual connection, read some degree of body language – even if it's only the top half of the body – and present yourself as more than just a voice. You may be able to see people's facial expressions, but it is a lot harder to read the room or get energy from those listening to you. So, to be successful, you will have to work just a little harder and be just a bit more prepared.

Situational analysis dictates you do your homework. Google participants when possible check out the company and the industry, gather whatever information you can before your conversation. Get a snapshot on current events. If there is something going on in the world of significance on that day you will be prepared to formulate a

[5]Mehrabian, Albert, 'Some Referents and Measures of Nonverbal Behaviour', Behavior, Research, Methods and Instruments, 1969, Vol.1 (6).

comment or opinion. This information may never come up, but you will be read in the moment.

A Zoom meeting or a Teams call, or a Webex session, is basically live broadcasting, so anything can happen. Plan your presentation. Look at your background. What does it say about you? There is a reason that during COVID-19 when so many of the interviews on news channels were done from people's homes, you saw a lot of bookshelves. We associate books with credibility, making it a perfect nondescript, but smart backdrop. Think about how you look. Take a moment to view yourself in advance and make sure your camera lets you make the point you want to make. All this helps you through that most awkward early part of a video call. It may also boost your self-confidence and let you take command of the situation, allowing you to ask thoughtful, relevant questions and engage intelligently.

Think of one of the most popular and pressure-filled uses of video communication – the job interview. It just makes sense that as companies search the globe for candidates, they choose to use video rather than phone in the early rounds. The shift to remote work with the COVID-19 pandemic rocketed up video interviewing in 2020 and 2021 by more than 500 per cent, but even before then, the rates were steadily climbing and will likely increasingly become the norm.[6] Those who are hiring get the chance to see you, hear your immediate responses to questions and study mannerisms that experienced HR people and recruiters know how to interpret. And now that so much business is done remotely, they will also be judging your telegenic abilities.

Whether it is the improved technology or an interest in controlling hiring costs, video interviews have become much more important in the hiring process.[7] In the past, phone or video interviews were used in the culling process. Once applicants passed the resume test,

[6]Steinberg, Scott (24 May 2020), 'Coronavirus Hiring: How Recruiters Are Selecting and Interviewing Job Candidates during the Pandemic', CNBC, https://www.cnbc.com/2020/05/24/how-recruiters-select-and-interview-job-candidates-amid-coronavirus.html
[7]Joshi, Aparna et al. (1 September 2020), 'Video Interviewing: A Review and Recommendations for Implementation in the Era of COVID-19 and Beyond', *Academic Radiology* 27, No. 9: 1316–22, https://doi.org/10.1016/j.acra.2020.05.020

recruiters would move to these tools to move them to the next step: the in-person interview. With more widespread use and greater social acceptance of video, it is no longer just a primary tool for rejection and elimination of applicants. Thus, it behoves both applicant and recruiter to use the technology effectively, so the best candidates are recruited.

Although video interviews have and will likely continue to be used in job interviews, research indicates there are definite drawbacks with video communication over face-to-face interviews. Baker et al. found that face-to-face interviewers perceived participants as 'more experienced, thoughtful, competent, experienced and intelligent'. Interviewers using video perceptions were added more negatives. They described participants as 'thoughtful and intelligent' but more often as 'unprepared, unenthusiastic, uninterested and bored'.[8]

So, although the rules for a good video interview are pretty much the same as for in-person, the research indicates people tend to forget them when using technology. So, let us remind you here.

Simple is always better. As with any job interview, shorter answers are always preferable. You'll want to speak clearly and succinctly. Rambling in an interview is always problematic, but on video, it can be easier to go down the rabbit hole with only facial cues from the interviewer. To that end, you should always prepare a short list of written bullet points, a kind of personal cheat sheet, so you know the points you want to make before you start the video interview. You are far more susceptible to distraction in a video interview than sitting in the hiring manager's office. Every bird sound, every incoming email alert, every twist of your chair, every visual or technical hiccup can take you off your game, affecting both your messaging and your credibility.

There is a tendency for us to want to think of doing a video interview in the same casual way we take a phone call. That is a bad idea. In fact, neither should be approached casually. One of the most

[8]Baker, D.A., Burns, Devin M. & Reynolds Kueny, Clair (16 August 2020), 'Just Sit Back and Watch: Large Disparities between Video and Face-to-Face Interview Observers in Applicant Ratings', *International Journal of Human–Computer Interaction*, 1–12, https://doi.org/10.1080/10447318.2020.1805874

important factors to focus on is energy. When we coach someone on how to be most effective on a phone call, we generally tell them to get up and pace around the room while talking. It brings energy to your voice to be upright and moving around and allows your mind to focus better. A video conversation requires the same level of energy and concentration to put your thoughts together, but you're restricted by the physical construct and you can't utilize either of these important practices. The result is maintaining energy and enthusiasm can be a huge challenge, especially on a video call that goes on for more than a half-hour.

Building energy in a video call means that you have to do it without being able to move your body. So, what you want to do is move your hands. Gestures, even those the others on the video call cannot see, add energy to your voice. Make sure your hands are not clasped or otherwise engaged. Try to keep them away from your face. It is distracting and often appears like you are having to hold your head up. Keep your arms free with enough space around you so you can gesture without putting your water or coffee in danger.

Focus and engagement add complexity in a video interview because you are always on. The camera is on you even if you are part of a group interview and you aren't speaking at that moment. There are no off-camera moments when you can let your interest wane. In a video panel interview with participants all in little boxes, you cannot go wrong if you just assume someone is watching you all the time. When you speak, look at the camera. The temptation is to look at the people, but then you do not look as if you are looking at them. An external camera that can be angled right over the screen will give you the illusion of looking at it when you are looking at the other participants. With an internal camera, you reduce the size of the participant boxes and drag them up directly under the camera. Your eyeline diversion at that distance is almost indistinguishable and this way you can see people while still giving the impression that you are looking directly into the camera.

Of greatest importance is to avoid looking at yourself. That will take your attention away from the people you should be watching – the others on the call. Additionally, it can help you avoid the temptation to fix your hair or adjust your shirt. Such fussing and primping on camera is distracting and demonstrates a lack of interest in others. It can also trigger a kind of mirror face, that involuntary look people often make in front of a mirror – a pose or expression that really isn't natural and doesn't work well on a video call. Some video platforms give you the option to turn off your self-view. If you find yourself distracted, consider using it!

There are a few basic things we can all do to improve the quality of the physical and audio of our video communications. In this case, borrowing from TV, motion picture production and set design can prove useful and effective.

First off, test your internet connection. Video is still the biggest hog of bandwidth. Make sure you have enough to spare. Test out everything in advance and that doesn't mean five minutes before, especially if you are asked to log in to a video chat platform with which you are not familiar. Some platforms perform better on different browsers. What might work great on Chrome could fail, or have limited function, in Safari. Different platforms also utilize different scopes of vision available to your camera. One will feature you in a tight shot with little background exposure, while another may feature a wide angle that captures something in the room you would rather not show. The only way to be sure is to test in advance and make appropriate accommodations.

Think of your camera and base location as your storefront window, where whomever you're speaking to is looking to buy what you have to sell: namely you. There is no additional opportunity to direct emotion or highlight any aspect of your personality with the camera. When you start your call, the mind takes in the full picture of whatever image you choose to project within the space, then you immediately want the conversation to focus completely on you. More and more participants are using virtual backdrops to avoid having to worry about what is seen in a home or office. That is fine, but consider the message you want to convey in even that selection. Often people are using the before-mentioned bookshelves image, others however are opting for more whimsical backdrops like beach scenes or family photos. Just be aware that your choice will create some physical context to your conversation and will be a perpetual reminder of how you want to be perceived.

What you generally want to have is a mini-set that conveys what you want the viewer to believe is an extension of who you are, or at a minimum not to challenge someone's abilities to concentrate on you. Remember, video communication is done with a fixed camera with a fixed angle. What you don't want is a background or atmosphere that's distracting as you cannot get a real read on the viewer's reactions. So, as a rule, whatever backdrop you choose, again, simpler is better. A real shelf with books, a small display, a healthy plant – but check the shot to be sure the plant doesn't look like it's growing out of your head.

Try to use the highest-quality video camera and audio available that you can afford. Avoid using your phone's camera unless you have a tripod and special microphone set up. Even some of the built-in cameras on most desk and laptops could use a serious upgrade. (Or at a minimum, a good cleaning.) There are scores of available small USB-HD cameras with better sound capabilities that will set you back less than £25 ($35). It's worth the investment.

Is your lighting right? Never light from above or below, always choose eye-level, front-facing light. Never have a window or light source from behind, as it will blow out the picture. Perhaps consider purchasing an inexpensive ring light to ensure flattering lighting. Check the sound quality of your microphone and the quality of the acoustics in the room. Small computer mics are far less forgiving than the sound you can perceive by just having a conversation in the room. You might want to consider a better hardwired mic or even a headset, if you don't mind the call centre operator look. In general, rooms with furniture, rugs, drapes, and pictures are best because they absorb sound. These have the additional benefit of adding warmth and character to the room.

Consider the angle of the camera. If you are using a laptop, put it on a box or a stack of books so the camera at the top of your screen is at eye-level as you don't want the viewer to be looking at you up your nose. For business communications, men and women should both wear make-up. These days, no one wants to go in front of any camera without at least a small amount of face powder to avoid looking 'shiny' and nervous. Again, it's not about trying to be something you're not, it's about removing distractions and negativity that will get in the way of who you are.

Dress to impress, or at least keep it in line with the tone and (in)formality of the conversation. Be smart, just because you are communicating from home doesn't mean you should wear around-the-house clothes. Often whomever you're speaking with may be slightly jealous that you get to be at home and they have to be in an office. It's generally an unspoken reaction, but a real one and there is no need to rub it in by being too casual and not appearing to care.

Your wardrobe and your visual image also go towards your credibility. Wearing the right clothes won't necessarily enhance your credibility, but the wrong clothes will certainly put a dent in it. And wear something presentable below the waist. I know, 'the camera will never see me', but you never know what could happen in the moment. Again, it's 'live' TV and it's a serious mistake if you have to react to a situation where it might become an issue.

In the end, how do you measure your personal success in video communications? You measure it in the same way as you measure your in-person communication: by the results. No doubt the process is different, but your aim is the same: to achieve your objective. Yes, it will require a bit more focus and a different kind of planning but your serious approach to this powerful communication tool will yield great personal and professional dividends.

VIDEO TIPS FOR YOUR COMMUNICATION STYLE

How You Prepare Information	
Meticulous	*Holistic*
What Likely Works for You	What Likely Works for You
Preparing is your superpower. This is especially useful in video meetings as it enables you to think through all of the unique elements that make video different from in-person communication. Use this as an opportunity to be strategic, considering all of the elements of video conferencing, not just your words.	Quick on your rhetorical feet, you are probably confident that whatever comes your way you will be able to handle it well. It is almost certainly true, but remember that video is different than in person and so give a little forethought to it. Yes, you can wing it, but there is less wiggle room in video. What could work in face-to-face communication may not be as effective in the virtual meeting or interview world.

What to Watch Out For	What to Watch Out For
Formulating your approach is all well and good, but you also want to be ready to react in real time. Assume someone will ask a question you did not foresee or present an unexpectedly harsh rebuttal. You cannot prepare for this, but you can remind yourself that you will be able to handle anything that comes your way, secure in the knowledge that your preparation will stand you in good stead.	It helps to remember that many video conference applications include recordings. It is likely that interviewers especially will take advantage in being able to review the interaction. This means you want to think about all of the elements of your online persona, including your background. What might not have been noticed during the video conference can become quite noticeable upon review. This is not the time to leave your credibility up to chance.

How You Convey Information

Direct	*Diplomatic*
What Likely Works for You	What Likely Works for You
Your frank approach to communication can work well when you are in the virtual world. It enables you to convey candour despite the limitations of video. If you make sure your non-verbal communication is as upfront as your verbal, you should find your credibility capital is as strong on camera as it is in person.	Video is made for the diplomatic communicator because it shows how people are reacting to your message in a more focused view than you would get in a live interview or meeting. As long as you do not let their reactions throw you off your game, you can learn a lot. Use this to modify or elaborate your points and you can be extremely effective.
What to Watch Out For	What to Watch Out For
In the window of video meeting applications, don't forget that everything is magnified. This is especially so if you are having a small meeting or interview and your window is larger than the thumbnails found in larger groups. Additionally, when you are on speaker view, you fill the screen. Be aware of how this can make directness look like arrogance. Combine candour with charm and you will find your credibility can go off the charts.	The challenge of focusing on how others are responding to your message is that it can distract you from your message. While you want to be able to use their reactions to adapt, if you begin to concentrate on every little fidget, you will likely lose your train of thought. Don't overthink and you will find their reactions can help, not hinder, your connection with your audience.

How You Receive Communication	
Relational	*Substantive*
What Likely Works for You	What Likely Works for You
Your active listening proclivities stand you in good stead in the virtual world. Paying attention to all of the signals people give off will give you a sense of their perceptions. People like it when audiences show they are taking note of their communication. This is something you do naturally and helps build your credibility capital.	Content is king to the substantive communicator and that is what you listen for in a video conference. You are less likely to be distracted by the setting or other extraneous activity. This allows you to pay close attention to the gist of the matter.
What to Watch Out For	What to Watch Out For
Don't let your focus on how they are communicating to you get in the way of heeding the actual content. Process the details. Listen carefully to their arguments and explanations. After all, you have points you want to make and you need clarity on theirs to be successful.	Yes, you listen for the content, but you mostly care about what is in keeping with your interests. Let your attention wander, however, and you are going to find yourself in trouble. First of all, on video losing focus is all too noticeable. Second, given your penchant for planning your responses, this will take your attention away from the discussion as well. So, avoid doing that. Even if the topic has become boring to you, don't take a mental vacation. You never know when it is going to take a turn that will make the topic of conversation of critical importance to you and what you want to achieve.

How You Relate to Others	
Collaborative	*Independent*
What Likely Works for You	What Likely Works for You
While video conferencing is certainly different from in person, it still provides you with the opportunity to connect and build relationships. Given that these are your natural inclinations, take advantage of them in the virtual world. Show your warmth. Demonstrate your empathy. People will appreciate it and your credibility will reflect that.	Some people may be more reticent to speak up in video meetings. After all, there are a lot of people looking at you in a more pronounced manner than what you would experience around a conference table. This is not an issue for you. Your commitment to stand up for your ideas and perspectives is going to outweigh any concerns about all the faces on your computer screen.

What to Watch Out For	What to Watch Out For
It's not selfish to have your own goals and objectives. You do not always have to put everyone ahead of yourself or their interests ahead of your own – even on video. You might feel uncomfortable when people go to their argumentative corners. This may make you retreat. Don't. Video focuses attention on your facial expressions. Keep yours open. Keep yours engaged. This will give you the relational space to support consensus, but not at the expense of your own interests.	Defend your ideas? Of course, but remember that on video you may seem more belligerent than assertive. The spotlight intensifies facial expressions. What might be regarded as concentration face to face may well seem belligerent on video. Don't chance conflict. Breathe. Smile. Your credibility will take a hit if you are seen as aggressive and aloof.

Your Communication Personality

Animated	*Controlled*
What Likely Works for You	What Likely Works for You
You are a natural for video. Your natural style conveys warmth and charm. This really takes advantage of the richness of the medium. Expressive communication can reach out from the screen and pull people in. You can make them feel as if you are right there with them. That is a great credibility advantage to have.	Calm, cool and collected can be an asset, even on video. You prefer smaller gatherings and you can make video feel like this by what you show on screen. Fifty people make you uncomfortable? Show only ten – but make sure it is the right ten! This can make you feel more in control and that will in turn increase your credibility.
What to Watch Out For	What to Watch Out For
Yes, video likes you. Yes, your expressiveness is an advantage. But be aware that there is still a difference from in person. If you get overly excited, it may not take much to be over-the-top on video. So, pull it back a touch. Don't try to be something you're not but pay attention to the medium. The screen is smaller – your expressiveness needs to be a little smaller, too.	Keeping people's attention is always a challenge in this overstimulated world, online just makes it worse. People can look as if they are paying attention but they are really doing something else. Don't make it easy for them. Work on getting some variety in your voice. Make your slides interesting. Use stories. You might feel a bit uncomfortable at first, but then if you aren't feeling a bit uncomfortable, you aren't growing as an effective and credible communicator.

15

Acing Interviews

Congratulations! You've been offered an interview. There is no better way to showcase your credibility on a topic than in an interview. While most people do not get their 15 minutes of fame on a major television or cable channel, many are interviewed for company or organization publications – paper or digital. The advice applies to both.

Here is the good news about interviews: the act of being put on the spot to come up with answers is actually a gift. Generally speaking, freezing up is rare and only occasionally do people really regret something they said. So, relax. An interview can be a liberating experience that can bring out the best in you.

THE VIDEO INTERVIEW

While it might seem that the interviewer is in control, in reality the opposite is true. Yes, the interviewer is asking the questions, but the subject – and the knowledge and expertise they have to offer – is the entire reason for the interview in the first place. That puts the power squarely in the subject's court.

There are various kinds of video interviews with which you are probably familiar, starting with the ubiquitous celebrity interviews on commercially broadcast talk shows. Don't be fooled, though: those appearances are rarely actual interviews. They are pre-produced, entertainment presentations designed to promote someone's career, new book, surprising achievement or an upcoming performance or appearance. The host is playing the role of an interviewer, making the conversation appear fresh and interesting, but that's only the tip of the iceberg. In reality, what you see on air is the result of a team of producing professionals whose full-time job it is to make the host look good and sound intelligent. Such is the world of ratings and job security for the producers. These TV appearances have got shorter as producers have learned that viewer attention span has shortened over time: a Microsoft Canadian study suggested attention spans are down to a mere eight seconds.[1] That might just be a little pessimistic, but it is true that TV talk shows tend to stack their shows with a third more guests than just a few years ago. And the proliferation of easy to book, minimal quality zoomed-in video interviews have created even less opportunity for 'genuine' moments. Hence, what appears to be spontaneous and extemporaneous is not. So, in that sense, TV News interviews are not particularly helpful if you are looking for tips on

[1]Microsoft attention spans, Spring 2015, https://dl.motamem.org/microsoft-attention-sp ans-research-report.pdf

how to give a successful business interview. But, on the chance that you are asked to be a source for a news video interview, understanding how they work can be useful.

Typical on-camera reporters, even in major markets such as Los Angeles and New York, are essentially one-person bands. With the exception of a camera person to handle the technical aspects of a shot, the reporter is researching, booking, producing, editing and presenting the stories all on a short turnaround. These story presentations require interviews for credibility and pacing – this is where you would come into the picture. Certainly, there continues to be longer investigative pieces in the tradition of news magazines like *60 Minutes* or *Dateline*, but these require a different mindset and should only be considered with the right degree of thought and counselling. Those shows adhere to tight standards and base their credibility on a style you can easily research, but as they have the 'final cut', interviewees will always be at their mercy. If you should ever find yourself requested for an interview with one of the news magazines, think carefully. Those pieces are the result of in-depth research and you might find yourself more in a more adversarial environment than you expected.

There are specific physical and logistics to video, print, podcasts and radio interviews, but the core of your process should remain consistent. Here are a few general rules for any kind of interview. Follow them and you are likely to emerge unscathed.

HAVE A PURPOSE

Know your goal. Understand what points you want to cover and how they support your goal. An ego stroke is not a good goal. Don't think of the interview as a personal validation, think of it as one stop on the road to achieving your purpose. Often, we've said to a client, 'Why are you even doing this?' This is an important question to ask, and if you can't come up with a satisfactory answer, don't do it. Remember, if you don't have a goal and specific language that you have considered to achieve that goal, don't bother wasting everyone's time.

The interviewer has a goal as well – after all, there is a reason they reached out to you. So, consider who they work for and the job they've been sent to do. They have a story in mind. Understanding that and helping them achieve their assignment, all while advancing your own goals, is the real measure of success. If your words are taken out of context by an ambitious writer, your credibility will be ultimate victim. As Sir Winston Churchill once said, 'You are the master of your unspoken words, but a slave to the words you have spoken.'

A quick review of almost any article, on-camera news story or podcast can reveal how an interviewer may use your quotes. The interviewer generally has in mind a journey on which they intend to take the reader or listener. But it's their road. Your primary function is that of a credible source. Quotations in articles are short, generally a mere one to three sentences, if that. These quotes are designed to help tell the narrative. To use a military analogy, some missions are about conquest and some are about escape. Interviews are best thought of as escapes. Point made. Successful extrication. No casualties. That's how we all live to fight another day. It's not a coincidence that on the day interviews come out, the predominant emotion a PR exec will express in private is one of relief, not jubilation. They know that exposure is always a risk/reward equation and to gain attention without humiliation or embarrassment is a victory in itself.

Don't worry about being thought of as a bad interviewee. You are expendable fodder for most reporters. They will get what they need from you (or your PR advocate) and move on. Even so-called relationships with journalists are based on a deal structure. You have something they want, and they have something you want in attention or notoriety for you, your service or your product – that's it. Beware of publicists, PR execs and communications specialists who claim to have great relationships with the press. At best, those are transactional and at worst, they are Faustian bargains. Remember, for most writers the focus is on their story, not on you or your team.

KNOWING YOUR INTERROGATOR
(UM, UH ... INTERVIEWER)

Once you have agreed to an interview request, don't rest on any laurels. Understand the interviewer, their style, their approach, their reputation. Do your homework. Are you being interviewed for some supplemental quotations, or are you the focus? Could you be walking into a trap? Interviews are like an open book test. There is absolutely no reason to fail in this world of the internet. Journalists are for the most part transparent. In a society where journalist branding is almost a must, it's generally easy to assess where they're coming from and what kinds of stories they are most likely to tell about you. Just like doctors, the trend among journalists is away from generalists and more towards specialists. Journalists have a voice and they write with personality. Understand that voice and personality and you will have all you need to know about what box they want your interview to fit into.

Remember, if you smell a rat, there's a pretty good chance there is one around. If you think you might be walking into ambush – a term that emerged from early *60 Minutes* interviews – don't do the interview. If you think you will be able to dazzle them with your style and charm, forget it. You might think you've prepared extensively and followed through in the interview itself, but that is only the first part of the process. Having good instincts is part of why you are even in a position to be interviewed. Don't be taken in by your Communications or PR executives who are justifying their jobs by setting up interviews for you.

Steven had a client who was about to go on a nationwide investor/fundraising and media tour. He was the CEO and founder of a location-based mobile platform company that was revolutionary in the use of a phone's GPS, Wi-Fi and Bluetooth. The app would pinpoint your location in retail stores and make suggestions for items you might wish to purchase. The company had also just acquired a groundbreaking beacon technology company that further refined those capabilities. With a lot of buzz and enthusiasm for this improved service, the CEO was anxious to hit the road and tout these new sophisticated capabilities to retailers.

Kicking off the tour, their internal marketing department had set up an interview with the *Washington Post*'s chief tech reporting team, who had been working on a story about location tracking capabilities. And there is where goals diverged. The CEO thought he was explaining a breakthrough technology in marketing. He quickly learned that this story was going to be about the growing concern for personal privacy in the face of apps such as his. The marketing executive, anxious to deliver on her promise of national exposure, reassured the CEO that the writers were really interested in his advancements in maintaining anonymity and pinpointing locations so he agreed to be interviewed.

Steven was brought in to brief and prepare the CEO for the toughest of questions regarding the capabilities of the technology, the security safeguards and how the data acquired was actually being used. The interview itself went well. Afterwards, however, in subsequent deeper background conversations between the writer and PR firm, a different picture began to emerge. This was not going to be a story about how improved technology was going to make people's lives better, it was to be another example of how 'Big Brother' was taking another monumental step of encroachment. Both angles were accurate, but the tone and attitude of the story was proving to be the latter. In the end, the publicity exec was forced to beg the paper not to use the CEO's quotes. While not inflammatory when read independently, within the context of this investigative piece would have been the cause of much embarrassment and confusion for the platform, defeating the reason for the attention in the first place.

In his consulting and coaching, Steven would often find that clients let their enthusiasm for national exposure overpower everything else. They just forgot how easy it is to fall victim to the agendas of the publication and the journalist. It helps to remember that there is no interest from writers or readers in the proverbial dog-bites-man story. The scoop is the man-bites-dog story. So, understanding where the writer thinks the interesting approach is for a story is critical to ensuring you don't get bitten!

THE 30-SECOND RULE

A good rule of thumb is to avoid talking for more than 30 seconds at a time. Ask Siri or Alexa to give you a 30-second clock and see how long that feels. It's a long time. In fact, plenty of time to make a point. We incorrectly believe that a more complete answer will curry favour with the questioner and result in a more favourable overall result. Nothing could be further from the truth. In most cases, a questioner is looking for a succinct answer for their narrative, not a rambling, roundabout justification for a point that might be off the track of the original question.

In general, people feel very insecure about 'dead air', that uncomfortable silence after you have made your point. In fact, good reporters will stay quiet after you have said your piece. They know that you have probably planned a response or two to expected questions. They want that third or fourth answer that comes out spontaneous and unplanned. It likely won't support your goal, but it may be just the nugget they wanted for theirs.

The fear of dead air comes from sheer discomfort and insecurity that you haven't said the right thing. Manage that by becoming comfortable with the silence and staying focused on what you want to say and how you want to express it. There is a greater likelihood you will venture into the danger zone by over-answering than if you are just quiet. The longer you go on, the more likely you will either say something that you shouldn't, or you will invariably offer up a monologue from which the interviewer can cherry-pick something, take it out of context and twist the meaning of your answer. How do you prevent this? Stop talking! There is no guaranteed method, but the less rope you offer, the less chance you will be the victim of a hanging.

MAKE IT A TWO-WAY
(AKA WRITERS ARE PEOPLE TOO)

You want to be sure that you are engaging the interviewer. It's okay to compliment them and ask questions. In most cases it will endear you to them – unless you overdo it and become smarmy. This is the part we like to call *Writers Are People Too*. Your research will give you lots of question fodder. Cast aside the notion that you are going to charm them such that they will write glowingly of you, just treat them with respect and dignity. Think of this as a mutual aid agreement.

If you reach the highest heights of success, and are being interviewed because of your accomplishments, you may find yourself the object of envy. Writers are people, too; they might just have that tiny seed of insecurity themselves. This is not journalism at its noblest, but for a few, reporting on someone else's accomplishments can be demoralizing. The result can be a somewhat passive–aggressive approach to the interview. You may or may not be able to identify this approach, so stick to your plan. Use your research and focus on questions that relate to their research or general knowledge about the subjects you are discussing. These are all good topics of conversation.

ALWAYS-ON INTERVIEWS

Interviews don't just start when the reporter says, 'Okay, let's begin.' Every moment of the encounter is officially on the record. Nothing is off the record. Nothing. Zilch. Zip. Zero. Forget this at your peril. There is no warm-up, pre-interview time. No just getting-to-know-you intro. There are lots of stories of hot mics and what people – especially politicians – said when they thought no one was listening. It doesn't matter if it is in person or on the phone. Assume the virtual mic is always hot. After all, there are no interview do-overs. Knowing this means you have to be mindful of the interviewer themselves, as well as everyone else who is part of the process. Face it, Twitter, Instagram, Snap or Facebook are ubiquitous these days. If you are rude, supercilious, patronizing, inappropriate or demanding, it is honey to the social media bees. You will find yourself susceptible to ridicule and condemnation from these strangers. Assume everyone has an axe to grind and you'll be just fine. As Joseph Heller said in his World War II satirical novel, *Catch-22*, 'Just because you are paranoid, doesn't mean they aren't after you.' [2]

ENERGY AND BEING PHYSICALLY EXPRESSIVE

Your energy and enthusiasm will be infectious and will encourage an interviewer to match your passion. Your body language will play a large part in how you convey that interest. When you lean forward,

[2]Heller, Joseph, 1798–1849. *Catch-22, a Novel.* New York : The Modern Library, 1961.

the interviewer will want to lean forward. You have the power to set the physical energy as well as the emotional energy.

If you are on the phone, stand up. If you feel you must sit down, sit quite literally at the edge of your seat. If you are on a platform like Zoom, stand or sit forward and look at the camera – not at yourself. Give yourself every advantage to keep your energy up.

Where you sit can play a role in determining the dynamic of the interview. This is something called Power Sitting. During an interview we want the interviewer to feel at least like they are on common footing. Never give an interview from behind your desk. Not only is it off-putting due to the attempt to impress, but it also suggests a scenario where it appears you have something to hide. Using a massive piece of wood, stone or glass to serve as a barricade or shield can lead to an assumption you have something to hide. Power and dominance games almost always backfire. Trying to impress someone with who you are only challenges them to take the upper hand and we don't have to tell you who would come out on the losing end of that classic power struggle.

In the course of an interview, especially if it is long, you might find your energy beginning to lag. The result of that can be using filler words such as 'uh', 'um', 'like', 'you know' and the like, which can make you appear scattered and uncertain. The energy letdown can also cause mental stalls; you are thinking, but just a shade more slowly than ordinary. The solution is twofold. First, know your material backwards and forwards. People will cut you some slack and you don't have to be perfect, but reviewing and practising will always be your best weapon against these stalls. Second, take a second, a breath and think. That half-second break will give your brain a chance to recharge. These rules apply whether you are on camera, in person, or on the phone or a video conference tool.

DRESS TO BE COMFORTABLE AND APPROPRIATE

You have to be authentic to yourself, feel comfortable and consider how you want to be perceived while being interviewed. If perception is reality, how do you want to be perceived based on your appearance? Meaning, what do you want someone else's reality of who you are to be? One way to address this is in the selection of what you wear for an interview. It's not about buying a new suit or dress, although there is nothing wrong with a little retail therapy for a confidence boost. You want to think of your wardrobe as your costume for the reality of who you want to be and how you want to be perceived. The clothes you wear, the headshot you send out and the way you look should be a visual reflection of your best self. Don't rely solely on your own perspective. Seek out the advice of someone you trust so you will get the input to appear the most influential and credible person that you can be. Before you head out for the interview, make sure you look well-groomed. If wearing make-up it should be subtle and natural. And above all, you want your hair to be neat, combed and will stay that way.

WATCH THE HYPE

People notoriously run the extremes on this. They are either uncontrollable braggarts who are obsessed with sharing everything about what they have done so brilliantly, or so passive that the interviewer may feel getting anything out of them is like pulling the proverbial teeth. So, don't go to either extreme. There is an easy, comfortable medium: just mention what you are there to talk about twice. Mentioning it more than that may make you appear pushy and saying it less runs the risk of you not emphasizing your point – just do it in a way that is both organic and makes sense.

On the subject of word selection, in general we believe in keeping it simple. An interview is not the place to demonstrate your boundless vocabulary. A study by researchers at Carnegie Mellon found that most presidents use words consistent with 6th- and 8th-grade levels (a reading age of around 12 to 14 years).[3] This is a level that is accessible and easy to understand. The more complex your language and syntax, the more likely the chance for misunderstanding. If you are writing out your remarks – a questionable activity to begin with – read them out to someone and make sure you are making the points in the most

[3]Spice, Byron (16 March 2016), 'Most Presidential Candidates Speak at Grade 6–8 Level', *Carnegie Mellon University* (blog), http://www.cmu.edu/news/stories/archives/2016/march/speechifying.html

accessible way. Don't have them read it to themselves as that gives them more time to ponder the words than hearing them does. Better to write out an outline from which to practise. Your language will be more natural.

GOOGLE YOURSELF

The first thing any interviewer will do is Google you. So, you'd better Google yourself first. In fact, it is a good idea to do this periodically. If that is above your technical prowess, ask someone you trust to do it for you. If there's something that comes up that isn't accurate, you'll find it. This gives you the chance to set the record straight and alerts you to questions that might be asked.

Googling yourself is not a sign of vanity or narcissism, it's an accepted and encouraged practice just to be sure that there aren't stray rumours about you out there. You may think you aren't even famous enough to warrant a search. This is a fundamental error people make. The tentacles of the Web are more far-reaching than you know. Most people forget that photos, CVs, articles, casual mentions and any number of club and group listings are out there pretty much forever so don't bury your head in the sand assuming that what is out there is accurate and positive. If there is something negative out there – accurate or not – trust us, reporters will find it.

Google your name and it is likely you will find people who share your name, your birthday, your hometown. That leaves lots of room for confusion. It happens easily and journalists are no exception. You can't change the result of a Google search, but you can at least be aware of potential confusion and be ready to set the record straight.

CLOSING THOUGHTS

Don't think about 'winning' in an interview, survival is a more attainable goal. Your job is to be personal without being too revealing. Forthright, without feeling violated. Embrace the compliment of being interviewed, but don't get lulled into thinking that it's all about you. It's a complicated process, but you have the tools at your disposal to have the upper hand and ace this open book test.

INTERVIEW TIPS FOR YOUR COMMUNICATION STYLE

How You Prepare Information	
Meticulous	*Holistic*
What Likely Works for You	What Likely Works for You
You shine here because preparation is what you are all about. Thinking about what you want out of the interview is always appropriate. Just make sure you pay attention to what the interviewer wants out of the interview, too.	Your ability to think on your feet will serve you well during the interview. That looks and feels authentic and is engaging. Your flexibility will stand you in good stead no matter where the interviewer goes.
	What to Watch Out For
What to Watch Out For	Yes, you trust your ability to think aloud, but an interview may not be the best place to rely on that. Borrow a bit from the meticulous communicator and think about what you want to achieve and what might be the interviewer's agenda.
Interviews don't always go as the interviewee planned so don't get caught up in what you prepared for. Stay in the moment and be prepared for the unexpected.	
How You Convey Information	
Direct	*Diplomatic*
What Likely Works for You	What Likely Works for You
Your straightforward style enables you to respond to questions directly. Your focus is on the information and making sure it gets out.	Your focus on the audience facilitates building a relationship with them, in this case the interviewer. This permits you to get a sense of what is resonating and what might trigger some unexpected questions.
What to Watch Out For	What to Watch Out For
Candour is credibility building and one of your strengths. It is a two-edged sword, however, if you don't also pay attention to how your comments are being received. Watch the interviewer closely and you will be able to tell whether you are hitting home runs or foul balls.	The interviewer may seem receptive to your points and this can give you a false sense of confidence that you and they are on good terms. Don't fall for it. Pay as much attention to the kind of questions being asked and the direction the interview is taking as you do to the reactions to your answers.

How You Receive Communication	
Relational	*Substantive*
What Likely Works for You	What Likely Works for You
Actively listening and paying close attention in an interview is key to success. This permits you to focus your answers on what was asked and what might be behind it.	You focus on the task at hand and in the case of interviews that means what you planned to achieve. You listen with an eye on how to respond so that you move your points forward.
What to Watch Out For	What to Watch Out For
Just keep in mind that an interview is not any old conversation. No matter what kind of interview it is, remember your goal and why you agreed in the first place. One thing is certain, it is not to make a friend of the interviewer!	Staying connected to your points is all well and good, but remember, an interview is a two-person sport. Preparing your answers as the interviewer talks means you may miss critical points or worse, the focus of the question itself. Listen first, compose answer second should be your mantra.

How You Relate to Others	
Collaborative	*Independent*
What Likely Works for You	What Likely Works for You
Warm and empathetic, you can create a veneer of relationship with your interviewer. This can serve you well as long as you remember it is a facade. The interview is not about making a new friend, it is about getting your message out!	Lucky you, focusing on your interests is often your priority. You are clear on your goals and willing to defend your point of view in support of them.
What to Watch Out For	What to Watch Out For
Stay true to your goals and keep in mind that being liked by the interviewer is not one of them. Having a good connection to the interviewer is all well and good, but what people will remember is what you both said, not how friendly you were.	You are not conflict averse, so if you think you are being attacked, you are likely to react in kind. But don't. Listen. Take a deep breath, then marshal your thoughts, soften your voice and respond.

Your Communication Personality	
Animated	*Controlled*
What Likely Works for You	What Likely Works for You
You are a spirited communicator and that expressiveness can be a great addition to an interview. It makes you interesting and effective much of the time, just don't overdo it. After all, this is an interview, not a performance.	You like small groups more than huge audiences and in the case of an interview that can work for you. After all, in the moment it is just you and the interviewer and that can make you more comfortable.
What to Watch Out For	What to Watch Out For
You may run the risk of style over substance if you let your sparkling personality get the better of the interview. People may remember you as dynamic and spirited, but what you really want them to remember is your point of view. Don't sacrifice the latter for the former.	Just keep in mind that video or television can require just a little more oomph in your style than face to face, so you might want to remember that emotion and storytelling are powerful tools. Use them. And remember, smiling (when appropriate) works!

16

High Anxiety

Give people a choice between getting up in front of a group to present or going to the dentist – without anaesthetics – and you might be surprised how many will choose the dentist! It's often said that a fear of public speaking outranks even the fear of death. (The updated research is a little more precise in that fear of public speaking is the most *common* fear identified, not the top one for most people.[1]) Maybe it is because death seems a long way off, while presentations are a concrete, frequent and uncomfortably imaginable. Given no one has ever died, that we know of, from the process of giving a talk, the ubiquity of this fear is amazing. Certainly, not everyone has debilitating anxiety. We all know people who absolutely love public speaking. They might have been in competitive speech and debate in high school or college. They might have the performance gene that gives them endorphins from connecting with an audience. Or they just might have learned over time that this is something they do well and embraced it. If you are one of those lucky people, you are in the minority. For most, speaking in public, at least some of the time, is at best uncomfortable and at worst terrifying. Fortunately, after decades of helping people overcome this apprehension, we have learned a thing or two about the whys and wherefores of this phenomenon and, of much greater value to our clients and readers, how to overcome and manage it.

At some point almost everyone has experienced what James McCroskey called 'Communication Apprehension', or CA. McCroskey defines CA as 'fear or anxiety associated with either real or anticipated communication with another person or persons'.[2] Ever felt nervous about meeting the parents of a boyfriend or girlfriend? That was communication apprehension. Had that uncomfortable feeling walking into a party where you didn't know anyone? Communication apprehension. It is very common and over time we are usually able to come up with strategies to deal with it sufficiently to be able to get on with things. After all, you don't want to stop going to parties or meeting your significant other's parents. A subset of more generalized communication apprehension that we may encounter day-to-day is presentation anxiety, which is linked to the specific context and pressures of giving a more structured talk. We are often less equipped

[1]Kangas Dwyer, Karen & Davidson, Marlina M. (1 April 2012), 'Is Public Speaking Really More Feared Than Death?', *Communication Research Reports* 29, No. 2: 99–107, https://doi.org/10.1080/08824096.2012.667772
[2]McCroskey, James C. (2015), *An Introduction to Rhetorical Communication*, Routledge, https://doi.org/10.4324/9781315663791

to deal with it and it can be a challenge to overcome – that's what we'll focus on in this chapter.

One of the ways people often deal with communication apprehension is just to avoid the situations and interactions causing it altogether.[3] Tempting as this may be, it's not a sustainable or productive strategy. At best, it is career limiting and at worst, it can be career killing. That's especially true in today's work environment, where presentations are a near-inevitable fact of professional life across all manner of industries and careers. Once upon a work time, decisions were made on the basis of written materials. Memos and white papers and reports were the grist for the decision mill. Technology was, at best, telephonic and people read more than they talked and listened. So, presentation anxiety was much less of a career issue. That time is long gone. White papers have all but disappeared and memos are a thing of the past. With easy-to-use presentation software readily available, reports have been replaced with ubiquitous slideshows. Written arguments have been replaced by oral arguments. It might be a discussion around a conference table debating financial outlays. It could be a one-on-one meeting justifying a new hire request. It might be a campaign pitch to a client. It could be a program status report. It might be a presentation to the board of directors. Whatever it is, chances are it will involve you having to get up in front of an audience to speak. Avoidance is no longer a viable option. From classroom presentations to status briefings to pitching an idea, overcoming, or at least managing public speaking stress and anxiety is a key success factor for any career – and for your credibility. If you let communication apprehension get in your way, you may find yourself perceived by others as less credible and less influential.[4] Why give up valuable credibility capital for no good reason when there are strategies that you can use to effectively manage your anxiety?

Let's start by breaking down what communication anxiety actually is and where it comes from. Researchers distinguish between a few

---

[3]Ibid.

[4]McCroskey, James C. (2015), *An Introduction to Rhetorical Communication*, Routledge, https://doi.org/10.4324/9781315663791

basic types and sources of communication anxiety.[5] Anxiety could be linked to inherent elements of your personality. You might be shy and large groups make you feel uncomfortable, even when you know the people who are there. You may not like performing and find yourself feeling anxious when asked to do a reading in church or a toast at a wedding celebration. Personality-based anxiety will be fairly stable across multiple communication contexts. You can, however, learn to manage it.

Communication anxiety can also be situational. You may be a relatively relaxed speaker in informal settings, but a formal pitch to your boss, your boss's boss and your boss's boss's boss may send you into paroxysms of dread and terror. The difference in power dynamics can increase the intensity of your anxiety. In general, the idea that a single presentation will make or break your career lies primarily within your own mind. The more you believe you have riding on the outcome of any single presentation, the more likely you will find yourself feeling anxious – even if you are generally a comfortable public speaker.

An often-overarching element of public speaking fear is scrutiny anxiety. This one is pretty much what it sounds like: a fear of being judged and evaluated. It is a function of everyone's desire to be accepted, respected and, if not loved, at least liked. Conversely, it's also about fear of rejection. No wonder the greater the perceived stakes, the greater the fear of being judged and found wanting. In truth, it is exceedingly difficult to know exactly what is going on in the minds of your audience.

Human beings have a unique ability to envision that which does not exist. In the same way we can envision a future, we can envision

[5]Beatty, Michael & Behnke, Ralph R. (1991), 'Effects of Public Speaking Trait Anxiety and Intensity of Speaking Task on Heart Rate During Performance', *Human Communication Research* 18, No. 2: 147–76, https://doi.org/10.1111/j.1468-2958.1991.tb00542 .x; McCroskey, James C. & Beatty, Michael J. 'Oral Communication Apprehension', in *Shyness: Perspectives on Research and Treatment*, ed. Jones, Warren H., Cheek, Jonathan M. & Briggs, Stephen R. (1986), *Emotions, Personality, and Psychotherapy*, Boston, MA: Springer US, 279–93, https://doi.org/10.1007/978-1-4899-0525-3_21; Bodie, Graham (1 January 2010), 'A Racing Heart, Rattling Knees, and Ruminative Thoughts: Defining, Explaining, and Treating Public Speaking Anxiety', *Communication Education – COMMUN EDUC* 59: 70–105, https://doi.org/10.1080/03634520903443849

an event, or in this case, a presentation. Of course, we don't call it envisioning the future, we just think about what is going to happen – we plan. Unfortunately, for people who dread public speaking, all too often what is envisioned is failure, embarrassment and humiliation. The disasterizer in us assumes the worst, where all of the mental pictures of the upcoming situation are full of catastrophe, calamity and cataclysm. That's exceedingly unhelpful when trying to manage your anxiety because such negative thoughts and predictions can become self-fulfilling prophesies.

Self-fulfilling prophesies are a mental feedback loop between beliefs, behaviours and outcomes. Brandrick describes this as cognitive fusion, in which thoughts and feelings and visions are responded to as if they are real, factual and true.[6] These prophesies of the future become self-fulfilling if you are focused on them when you should be planning, preparing and practising. If your thoughts are full of fears of embarrassment when presenting, you will find yourself presenting with your thoughts being more on yourself and your fears rather than on your material, your arguments and your audience. That focus, in turn, will likely mean your presentation becomes the disaster you predicted. In fact, research shows that those who are more anxious about speaking tend to be more self-focused – that is, they pay more attention to their own feelings and fears than those for whom public speaking is less anxiety producing.[7]

Some of these questions of self-doubt are related to your physical presentation. Luckily, these are easily monitored and corrected. Did you dress appropriately? Did they notice the coffee stain you got on your jacket right before entering the room? Do the slides look right? Did you drop your notes? The good news is while no situation is ever perfect, you are most likely fixating on things no one in your audience ever will. That also means when you make a mistake or leave something out of your presentation, 99 per cent of

[6]Brandrick, Chloe et al. (6 October 2020), 'A Comparison of Ultra-Brief Cognitive Defusion and Positive Affirmation Interventions on the Reduction of Public Speaking Anxiety', *The Psychological Record*, https://doi.org/10.1007/s40732-020-00432-z

[7]Deiters, Désirée D. et al. (1 June 2013), 'Internal and External Attention in Speech Anxiety', *Journal of Behaviour Therapy and Experimental Psychiatry* 44, No. 2: 143–9, https://doi.org/10.1016/j.jbtep.2012.09.001

your audience will never know unless you decide to tell them. So, don't. Just go on.

Communication anxiety is primarily a mental phenomenon that manifests itself physically so it is important to first understand this intertwined relationship before we go into how to overcome it. After all, we tend to describe the physical elements more than we take notice of the mental.

Most of us have an inner voice that makes its home inside our heads. Sometimes called self-talk or inner dialogue, it is that little voice that goes on and on in our heads, a kind of running commentary of our lives. Researchers describe it as 'a platform for observing, monitoring, and directing one's own behaviour'.[8] It is what you hear in your head when the grocery line next to you goes faster than the one you are in – 'should have gotten in that line!' It can manifest itself differently in different people, but it is a way of processing information and experience – past, present and future. It is part of our planning process. While most people do this in language, not everyone has an internal dialogue. Some people experience it in a less explicit, conceptual, non-language process. However the process unfolds, our integration of the world around us and ourselves begins here. It is also where communication anxiety originates. For people with communication apprehension that little voice can create a self-critical minefield. Just outlining the talk or creating the slides gives rise to images of bored audiences, harsh questions, ignored jokes and generally desultory reactions. The more these images take hold in our minds, the more anxiety builds and the more apprehension grows.

Negative self-talk is self-critically looking back at the past and forward into the future. But self-talk does not always have to be damaging or unconstructive. With positive coping and learning mechanisms that allow you to reflect, respond and react, it can also be a reinforcing, self-managing approach to problem solving and a kind

[8]Shi, Xiaowei, Brinthaupt, Thomas M. & McCree, Margaret (1 March 2015), 'The Relationship of Self-Talk Frequency to Communication Apprehension and Public Speaking Anxiety', *Personality and Individual Differences* 75: 125–9, https://doi.org/10.1016/j.paid .2014.11.023

of social assessment for reviewing interactions.[9] It may not feel like it, but you have control over this mental phenomenon.

It rarely works to try and block it or just tell yourself to calm down. Instead, you want to deliberately recalibrate how you respond to your thoughts about an experience, past or future. Already you know that you should remove language like 'embarrassment', 'fail', 'stupid' and 'can't' from your self-talk glossary. These words literally drag you down so replace them with positive and empowering terms. Notice when your little voice goes negative when putting a presentation together, then reframe that thought. This isn't a simple task because for it to work, you have to be willing to believe you can succeed. Knowing that the experts have your back and there is extensive evidence of this kind of mental reframing can be very effective.[10]

No one wants to fail, yet it is ridiculously easy to imagine it and the consequences that follow. It's infinitely harder to envision success and its subsequent enjoyment, so work at it. Give yourself credit for your innovative ideas. Be kind to yourself when assessing your preparation. Remind yourself there is a reason you were asked to make this pitch and embrace your own expertise. In general, your credibility has brought you to this place of authority from which you can present your point of view. Of course, if your presentation topic has opposition from members of the audience, they may not be rooting for your success. But that is political, not personal. They are going to be focused on your arguments and how they might counter them, not the number of times you said 'uh' or 'um'.

Communication anxiety is a mental phenomenon that manifests itself physically. It's often these symptoms that we notice most: the increased heartrate, rapid breathing, clammy hands, nausea,

[9]Shi, Xiaowei, Brinthaupt, Thomas M. & McCree, Margaret (1 March 2015), 'The Relationship of Self-Talk Frequency to Communication Apprehension and Public Speaking Anxiety', *Personality and Individual Differences* 75: 125–29, https://doi.org/10.1016/j.paid.2014.11.023

[10]Wood Brooks, Alison (2014), 'Get Excited: Reappraising Pre-Performance Anxiety as Excitement', *Journal of Experimental Psychology: General* 143, No. 3: 1144–58, https://doi.org/10.1037/a0035325

dizziness.[11] Some people turn red, others find their hands or legs start to shake. These are not imaginary responses, but they can be managed. It may help to remember that whether mental or physical, most of these elements of communication apprehension are invisible to the observer. Even shaking legs or hands are slight movements that rarely call attention to themselves.

You, however, are feeling these things and just telling yourself the audience won't notice may not put you more at ease. So, fight fire with fire. Taking deliberate physical steps to counter these physiological effects actually works. Deep breathing is inherently calming. It fools the body, and the mind, into thinking that it is no longer in fight or flight mode. Breathe in deeply for a count of four. Hold your breath for another count of four and then breathe out slowly for a count of eight. Repeat. Isometric exercises help relax both your body and your mind. Clench and unclench your stomach muscles by tightening your abs. Making fists and letting them go can help as well. Notice the feeling of relaxation when you let go. Take a sip of water. Smile! It relaxes your face and you.

There is one more trick you can use to banish the audience's perception of your public speaking comfort: just pretend you are comfortable and in charge. That may sound glib, but there's real substance to it. One of the cruel jokes of the universe is that the observable things you do to make yourself feel more comfortable when presenting often communicate nervousness to the observer. We discuss this in detail in Chapter 8 on Non-Verbal Communication (*see also* pp. 96–111), but it is worth a reminder here. Putting your hands in your pockets, clasping hands behind your back, folding your hands together in some kind of death grip all communicate nervousness, creating a vicious feedback loop between your mental and physical state. But the converse works as well. So, stand straight. Keep your hands in an open position. Smile. Focus on your topic, your point of view, your argument. Look as if you are enjoying the public speaking process and you might find you actually are. But even if you are not, the audience will think you are and that perception can become your reality.

[11]McCroskey, James C. (January 1976), 'The Effects of Communication Apprehension on Nonverbal Behaviour', *Communication Quarterly* 24, No. 1: 39–44, https://doi.org/10.1080/01463377609369208

Throughout her career, Rebecca coached many an executive along with thousands of students. Helping them overcome communication apprehension was a big part of a lot of these interactions. When a presenter would hold a pen, or lean on a lectern, or fold their arms, she would ask them why they did it. Inevitably, they would explain it made them more comfortable.

Her reply? 'My PhD is in communication, not psychology. I don't care how you feel, I care how you look!'

When the laughter subsided, she could explain why.

And then there is always familiarity with the material. A key source of apprehension and anxiety comes from a lack of practice and ownership of the content – straining to remember what your next slide or struggling to find the best way to convey a key concept will only heighten stress unnecessarily. Whatever your tried-and-true notes/script technique is, you can remove a significant layer of anxiety by simply creating a bulletproof knowledge of the subject.

Practise these techniques and you'll start notice a real difference in your anxiety levels. And know that the more you do it, the more comfortable it will get. Scholars call the treating anxiety with exposure to a trigger 'habituation', which is really a variation on the old saying, 'That which does not kill us makes us stronger.' A study by Finn, Sawyer & Behnke should give hope to all who fear public speaking that it really can get easier. The study found that just continuing to do public speaking, that is habituation, worked to reduce public speaking anxiety.[12] The more you put yourself in the position of presenting, the more you will increase your confidence and comfort level. In the immortal words of Nike, just do it!

Managing and overcoming the vicious cycle of communication anxiety requires you to be vigilant and notice when thoughts that feed unproductive anxiety pop up, cycle, expand and pop-up again. You want to see these thoughts for what they are, just thoughts. No

[12]Finn, Amber N., Sawyer, Chris R. & Behnke, Ralph R. (1 September 2003), 'Audience-perceived Anxiety Patterns of Public Speakers', *Communication Quarterly* 51, No. 4: 470–81, https://doi.org/10.1080/01463370309370168

reality, no mass, no predictive value unless you give it to them. So, don't. Replace them with more positive self-reinforcement. After all, you are most likely making up the negative forces, so why not create positive forces that move you forward to success rather than backwards into failure?

MANAGING ANXIETY TIPS FOR YOUR COMMUNICATION STYLE

How You Prepare Information	
Meticulous	*Holistic*
What Likely Works for You	What Likely Works for You
Your detail-oriented approach likely results in great preparation for your presentations. Not only do you have the slides but back-up slides for back-up slides. Lean into this tendency to manage communication anxiety with preparation and practice. Your goal of not being surprised by any opposition helps keep the disasterizer in you at bay.	Your big picture approach to life in general and communication in specific means that for the most part, you may not be particularly prone to communication anxiety because you figure you can go with the discussion flow. Question and answer may be your favourite part of a presentation because success requires the quick-thinking and flexibility you consider your strength.
What to Watch Out For	What to Watch Out For
While preparation to combat anxiety is important, you also need to be able to think on your feet. Practise speaking spontaneously in situations that give you the opportunity but are not high career stakes. Take a moment and think. Focus on the thought you want to communicate rather than the wording. And remember, no one ever died because they responded to a question without the perfect wording.	The ability to think on your feet is a great resource to have in your repertoire, but it should only be one of many. Planning may not be your first instinct, but you need to make it one of your top five. Take the time to think through your presentation. While slides can be overused, they are expected and used well, can be quite persuasive. Ironically, your relative lack of communication anxiety can be problematic: if you have unbridled faith in both your comfort level and your abilities, you may well think planning is both unnecessary and a waste of valuable time. In both cases, you will be wrong.

How You Convey Information	
Direct	*Diplomatic*
What Likely Works for You	What Likely Works for You
The more direct you are, the more likely it is that you are comfortable presenting and defending your ideas. You may still feel those butterflies in your stomach, but the situation is more important and you find yourself forgetting them. This gives you a definite edge over your more reticent colleagues.	If you are naturally more diplomatic, you may have certain advantages over your more direct colleagues – if you can overcome your own communication anxiety. You pay attention to what others say and how they say it and you work at acknowledging that. You are tactful. You use qualifying phrases which create space for others to present their positions. By focusing on how others are reacting rather than how you are feeling, you may well find you cease to notice your own anxiety. Which, in turn, increases your credibility capital.
What to Watch Out For	What to Watch Out For
There is another side to this coin, however, and it is worth remembering. Your confidence may well be off-putting to others if you run roughshod over their perspectives so pay close attention to how others are reacting. Their communication anxiety may impede their rebuttals to your arguments, but that silence may not mean you have persuaded them to your point of view. Indeed, you may have influenced them, but not in the direction you intended.	Wanting to be diplomatic when you feel strongly about an issue may make you concerned that you will rub others the wrong way if you argue vigorously. You might fear they will turn around and attack you and your ideas, so question and answer formats can exacerbate any and all presentation anxiety you already feel. You will likely discover your fight or flight instinct is to flee screaming in such instances. Don't. Take that deep breath. Listen closely. Remember, yours is an innovative idea and stay focused on that. Yes, you will want to do this in your diplomatic way – but do it.

How You Receive Communication

Relational	*Substantive*
What Likely Works for You	What Likely Works for You
Paying attention to how others are reacting to your presentations can help you feel less anxious. Remember, that anxiety means your attention is on yourself rather than those listening to you. So, if you work to interpret the non-verbal signals indicating what is happening in your listeners' minds, you are less likely to be focused on your own discomfort.	Given that you are focused on the information you are presenting, this may help you feel less anxious. You narrow your attention to the materials and that requires a lot of concentration, which can in turn crowd out the self-focused thoughts that trigger anxiety.
What to Watch Out For	What to Watch Out For
Figuring out how your messages are landing is all well and good, but you may find yourself stuck in the middle of your talk if you see people reacting negatively. Shaking their heads, whispering among themselves, writing notes are all signs an empathetic listener will notice and interpret. This, in turn, can send you into paroxysms of anxiety. So, take advantage of noticing and stop and ask questions. You may be able to get important feedback to which you can immediately respond – which, of course, will build credibility capital.	Focusing on the content can be a kind of self-tricking mechanism in which you basically pretend the audience are passive absorbers of your information. This can be risky because, let's face it, they are not. If you are not able to identify or at least notice the audience's reactions, you may find yourself facing a number of unpleasant surprises at the end of your talk. To avoid having this trigger your anxiety, do some preparation in advance. Try to identify the significant issues that could come up and think about how to present your replies. This gives you more of the content to focus on and will help you manage both your anxiety and your credibility capital.

How You Relate to Others

Collaborative	*Independent*
What Likely Works for You	What Likely Works for You
You value relationships and that can make you more outwardly focused. This is an advantage in managing anxiety because you are less likely to focus on what you are feeling than what others are.	You are all about winning. Your focus on your goals gives you confidence. And that is how you are likely to manage your anxiety. You are less concerned about others' reactions except in so far as they provide hints as to how to continue to build your arguments.

What to Watch Out For	What to Watch Out For
The advantages of this style can quickly become a presentation sand trap if you focus so much on others that their wants and needs take precedence over yours. If, however, you begin to feel you are not making progress in moving towards an understanding of your position or consensus, your attention can easily turn back to yourself, triggering what can be debilitating anxiety. So, stay externally focused. If you think the audience isn't with you, ask questions. Understand the sticking points, address them, but don't do it such that you put your own perspectives in peril.	As you are presenting and defending and you feel things are going your way, anxiety is reduced. So, you focus on your material. And that may work much of the time, but not always. Focusing on the material may mean it takes some time for you to realize if you are losing the room. That is uncomfortable, which in turn can trigger anxiety as you scramble to figure out what is happening and why. Content is not always king. People's reactions and perspectives matter, too. Thinking about that in advance, and a little while you present, may well help you both keep anxiety at bay and increase your credibility capital.

Your Communication Personality

Animated	*Controlled*
What Likely Works for You	What Likely Works for You
Your natural state is very expressive. You gesture, you move around, your face reflects what you are thinking and doing. This can help you keep anxiety at bay, or at least keep your audience from recognizing it. Your very animation communicates comfort, so make the most of that.	Your style is more subdued, so the audience is not expecting presentation fireworks. You don't show your feelings, but you have them. Your movements are there, but they are contained. You have positions and perspectives you care about, but you are generally reserved about them. People probably describe you as self-possessed. With your command of your content, and your restrained style, you may well be able to keep anxiety at bay, or at least not let it show.

What to Watch Out For	What to Watch Out For
The thing about communication personality is that it is unplanned and natural, it is just who you are. When, however, you are presenting and feeling nervous, your natural personality can go by the wayside. You start to focus on yourself and try to make yourself feel more comfortable. Your gestures become more restrained, your voice more measured, your words more guarded. This change in personality can call your entire presentation into question because, after all, you seem inauthentic. So, work to ensure that no matter what you are feeling, you do not let it show. Make sure your general dynamic personality shines through, no matter what is going on inside your head.	When you feel anxiety, your communication style may go from calm to catatonic. You pull inwards, but you really don't have much margin for error. When you are comfortable, you don't show much. When you are feeling nervous, you will likely show even less. This will make it extremely difficult to keep your audience's attention, or for that matter, make your points so work at building your body movement repertoire. Don't go overboard; that will be both extremely inauthentic and painful for you, but let your mind and body relax and focus back on your content. You just might finish the talk and barely realize you were nervous.

17

Putting It All Together

You have covered a lot of communication territory in the previous pages. Now is the time to think about how to put all of those concepts and topics into action. Your presentations, talks and speeches are the edge of the spear building your credibility capital. The best way to approach the presentation process is to think about it in three phases: before you deliver the talk, delivering the talk and the aftermath when your talk is concluded.

As you begin to plot your presentation journey, you'll want to remember that even more than your material, *you* are the star of the day. It doesn't hurt to think a bit about what gives celebrities that so-called 'star quality'. Basically, it comes down to three facets: appearance, talent and connection. Let's break it down.

APPEARANCE

This is not about beauty or handsomeness, it is about having a look that is both genuine and matches who you are and how you want to be perceived. It is about dressing to match the environment and the specific situation. You do not have to copy anyone, this is not about cookie-cutter dressing and looking like someone else. You do, however, want to ensure you are in the range of what they expect someone in your position to look like.

TALENT

Just being asked to give a presentation acknowledges your credibility and talent base from which to speak. It is a compliment! Your reputation and experience create an expectation that people will listen to what you have to say. Of course, this assumes you are speaking on a topic that reflects your experience, education and engagement. Always good to try to avoid faking it. Be true to what you know and who you are. Do not try to impress with exaggeration or implication; it never works and inevitably impacts your credibility.

CONNECTION

You make a connection with your audience by building rapport, so share a little bit of yourself in any talk. It highlights your humanness and enables people to see themselves just a little bit in you. It is the foundation of building trust with your audience.

So, before you begin, think about the talk in the context of these three elements. Make some notes with these facets in mind. As you go through the preparation process, keep coming back to those notes. You may add to them, alter or aggregate them.

The Before
As you begin to prepare the talk, a word to the wise. No one's career was ever ruined by one presentation, so don't send yourself into paroxysms of paralysis by making any one presentation more consequential than it is. That said, don't get over-confident and figure you can wing it either. Preparation is key to success. Remember that!

Before you start, think about the end. Remember the time after a presentation is always far longer and more significant than the presentation itself. Considering what you want people to remember afterwards is vital, so start with the result you want to achieve. Think about a two- to three-sentence recap that anyone in attendance should be able to recount. Think about it this way: if one of your attendees was in the lift with someone from another department and was asked about the meeting they were just in and the presentation they heard, what would you want the answer to be? Your job is to make sure they have a coherent summary in the time before the lift gets to the chosen floors. No doubt it will be short on details, but if you have planted a seed of authority and a key phrase or two, they should be able to give a cogent answer. That can create the kind of buzz that makes your credibility soar. The macro takeaway is always a good place to start. Once you have established that, then you can take a hard look at how to deliver the full talk to your audience.

Think about the venue in which you are speaking. Is it a large conference room? An auditorium? A small intimate room? The venue and the time of day you will present are certainly considerations. Keep in mind there is generally nothing you can do about either of these, but you can adapt to them. Whether your slot is first thing in the morning to a rested and fresh crowd of listeners, or you're speaking right after lunch or at the end of the day, your job is to be the best you can be, no matter where or when you go on. Do find out the basic physical and technical set up and your time limits, all of which will have a major impact on your talk.

The next step is conducting some basic audience analysis. Assess who they are, what their incoming perceptions are and what expectations they may bring with them. If it is an inhouse presentation to your colleagues and bosses, make sure you are clear as to what they already know and what their attitudes might be. A less-familiar audience of customers, clients or attendees at a convention means you may have to do more sleuthing. Figure out who are the most influential people there. Google them. Seek out LinkedIn profiles. You might even check out more social media such as Instagram or Facebook. Get the best feel you can for who they are and what they care about. The more you know about them, the more you can gear your talk to what will resonate best.

Give some thought to the corporate context in which you are speaking. Taking the temperature of a business environment will be a huge benefit. Pay attention to any rumours. Whether mergers or budget cuts, layoffs or share price, these will change the context in which your message is received. The more you know about the climate, the better off you are. And while you can't look into the minds of others, you start to understand what you think they will want or need to hear. Write these down. This will be useful when you begin to craft your talk.

Knowing your audience is something you likely do automatically every time you get together with friends and family. You know from experience what will push their emotional buttons and get a reaction; what will be well received and where there are land mines. With most presentations, you probably have a good handle on what you want or need to say. Don't over-rely on this, though. The key to your credibility is making sure you understand the audience's preconceived notions and how to address them, as well as anticipating the questions your talk will prompt. Once you have a handle on your audience, balanced with what needs to be said – and more importantly heard – then you are ready to write.

Writing Pains

If you are like most, writing is a chore, but take solace in this: when interviewed by acclaimed Hollywood director Martin Scorsese in the Netflix series *Pretend It's a City*, noted writer Fran Lebowitz declared, 'most people who love to write are horrible writers.' So, if in fact you dislike doing it, you might actually be rather good.

Not all presentations have the same weight and require the same level of analysis and preparation, but they all require forethought and some degree of homework so get underway by creating a list of the salient points you wish to make. Write them, dictate them, just get them out of your head … You'll find this cathartic in the sense that you won't be fixated on what you might be forgetting.

Once you have your list, number your points in the order that gives the presentation a logical flow. Every presentation is a story with a beginning, middle and an end. If you keep that in mind and consider that everyone is hearing this story for the first time, the order will come more naturally. Consider how you would want to be told the story if you were the listener. Your job is to have the most lasting impact, so don't worry about being too rudimentary in your telling of the story. Remember as a presenter you are taking them on a journey and you are the travel agent, chief tour guide, inn keeper and documentarian. It's your job to make the trip memorable – in a good way. You want to give them a headline, a map of the road ahead and a hint of what the conclusion will be. This engages your audience from the beginning.

Once your talking points are listed, start to flesh out the outline. This is for you alone – no one else will ever see it. This is not a word-for-word script. Unless you are giving a teleprompter address, writing out a talk is rarely a good idea. You want a guide for what you will say, but writing it out word for word can put your delivery at risk because the temptation to read rather than talk is overwhelming.

At this point in the process you are beginning to think about how you will create the road map for your presentation. Don't worry about making it too long – yet. Rather, you are building a deeper understanding of the material than you had at the start. Begin to think about the questions your listeners might have as they listen to you. You may well find yourself thinking about the material in ways you might never have anticipated. This will enable you to preempt the questions by making sure you address them within the presentation, which undoubtedly has a positive impact on your credibility capital.

The most effective talks are given in what we call a *USA Today*-newspaper language level. That national newspaper is written at a deliberately basic high-school reading level. This is not about talking down to your audience, it is about making sure there are no misinterpretations.

The first time Rebecca ran a survey at Hughes, she worked with a really terrific statistician whom we will call Joy. At the first project management meeting, Joy handed her a 6th-grade dictionary, aimed at 12-year-olds, and explained that any word not in that dictionary could not be in the survey. Rebecca was stunned because Hughes employees were highly educated and boasted a majority of employees with bachelor and post-graduate degrees. Joy explained that the more educated a person, the more likely they are to read more into the language used than is necessary. So, keeping the language at a relatively simple level ensured that people's interpretations as they answered the survey would be in sync. One example she gave is especially relevant in this book. When asking about how people felt about the various sources for information, Joy said the term to use was 'trust'. Rebecca had initially asked about which sources had the greatest credibility!

Projecting Yourself

One of the most often left-out parts of every initial draft is *you*. Whenever you engage with an audience, there are some go-to emotions that almost always engage the crowd. Make sure your arsenal contains personality, projection and promise. Use these well and you stand a good chance of your presentation achieving the desired results.

Being yourself is the platinum standard for credibility. Let your personality shine through. The worst mistake a speaker can make is to try to depersonalize the talk such that the presentation overwhelms who they are as individuals. You are delivering the talk for a reason, so don't try to hide behind the data and slides. Recall from Chapter 8 on Non-Verbal Communication (*see also* pp. 96–111) that how you use your voice matters. It signals to the audience how to process your information.

Personality is to a presentation what umami is to food – that subtle, almost invisible element which makes everything else more potent and impactful. This is where your trademark personal brand is so important. You might want to review Chapter 6 on your personal brand (*see also* pp. 71–82) and think about how yours will enhance your credibility and provide context and guidance for your listeners. This is what allows them to gauge the importance of the information. Without letting your personality shine through, you might as well just give them a handout of your points and let them come to their own conclusions. And that is never a recipe for success!

How your audience receives your personality comes through how you project it. People may be more or less animated (*see also* Chapter 1 and the Communication Self-Assessment, pp. 7–22), but as long as you project who you are with confidence, you will connect powerfully with your audience. In addition to how you use body movement, gestures and your voice (*see also* Chapter 8 on non-verbal communication, pp. 96–111), you want to be sure you are using language that will be persuasive to your listeners. Projecting your understanding of what is important to your listeners on the issue creates connection and builds credibility. They want to hear what you have to say and more importantly, how you say it.

The promise in every presentation or talk must be your authenticity. This builds trust and credibility. Even if your message is bad news – especially when it is bad news – you must show your authentic concern and understanding. If the reason for your talk is to present your approaches, ideas, recommendations and the like, you need to show that you are genuine in your belief that these will yield the desired and necessary results. This is the connection you always look to achieve in your talks.

The beginning of your talk sets the nature of the relationship you are building with your audience. Often people like to start a presentation with a joke or humorous story as an icebreaker. Not a bad idea in and of itself, but be aware that it should not be an ironclad rule. Your intro has to connect with the presentation, so a joke completely disconnected from your topic is apt to be unhelpful. Your delivery matters, too. We have all witnessed a speaker telling a joke at the outset of a presentation that bombed, embarrassing speaker and audience alike.

> Rebecca has a story she uses at the start of almost all of her talks: 'When I began at Hughes Aircraft, I had an early assignment with one of the senior scientists who helped invent geosynchronous communication satellites. Aerospace is one of the few industries that values PhDs and the scientist asked me, "I understand you have your PhD?" Well, it was still pretty new, and I was still pretty proud, and replied yes. At which point he asked what it was in. When I said communication, he asked if it was radio frequency or microwave. If I got a big laugh, I

would add, "Who knew microwaves communicated? I thought they just cooked!" I then said, "No, human communication." He looked at me quizzically and said, "They give a PhD in *that?*" Which is when I realized that in the Space and Communications Group where I worked, they were not talking about my kind of communication. At Hughes, satellites, antennas and computers communicated, people interfaced. So, I am pleased to tell you that today, we will talk about *my* kind of communication, the human kind!'

Luckily for Rebecca, almost any talk she gives focuses on communication, so this rather fun story applies in pretty much every situation.

There are other options besides humour. A simple lesson or shared personal moment that can resonate with an audience will go a long way towards getting started on the right foot. You might want to reread Chapter 7, Storytelling (*see also* pp. 83–95) and think again about how to find your stories. A word of advice, however: it is always good practice to test your ice-breaker story with a trusted friend or co-worker to see how it resonates within the context of your talk.

Be Your Own Editor

Once you have your story and methodology road map down, it's time to be your own editor. Remember, you are editing for content here, not wording. Editing can be a tricky thing. People are a little bimodal when it comes to this. Some feel every point is precious. Others are more pessimistic and are fearful much of their talk dismissed as inconsequential and they slash and burn content. The truth, of course, is somewhere in between. This is where you will want to go back to your original notes to see what was important to you at the outset. Your job is to be a credible communicator, not a preacher. It is a presentation, an act of communicating a message, not delivering a dissertation demonstrating how smart you are. In most situations less is more and simple is best. Remember, you are dealing with short attention spans no matter how proficient your audience is with any subject and how much they want or need to be engaged. Your being respectful of their time and capacity to listen will pay dividends in the long run.

As you review your document, one of the most basic editorial cuts you want to make is regarding industry jargon. There is a reason jargon is ubiquitous in organizations – it's an insider's communication shortcut. It may be okay, and even expected, to use some industry-related acronyms and insider phrases within your own presentation as long as you are sure everyone speaks that language. It doesn't take much for jargon to go from being an aid to effective communication to distraction and confusion. The secret to success is not only knowing your audience, but also understanding the knowledge base of that audience. This is an important part of the relatability issue we continually stress. It's not about finding the lowest common denominator in your language, it's about finding the strategic right blend that's the key. The demonstration of one's personal understanding, with the right mix of an objective industry perspective can be a great building block for credibility capital.

Engaging the Audience

Sometimes the most powerful part of your presentation is when you are not talking, so build some strategic silence into your talk. Most people seem to work hard to avoid dead air. This is unfortunate because there can be great power in not saying anything for a moment or two and letting the audience absorb and think. Nothing grabs people's attention more than unexpected silence. It is called a dramatic pause for a reason. That surprising quiet emphasizes critical points and commands attention in a way that sound cannot match. With silence, the audience immediately notices something is different and they sit up and take notice. Quiet is in almost everyone's wheelhouse and you can easily find the confidence to pull it off.

Throughout the presentation people want to have a sense of where you are in your story. It's not just about you when it comes to maintaining enthusiasm and energy, it's a two-way street if you don't just want to be listened to, but actually heard so keep them aware of where you are in the rhetorical journey. It helps if at the start you preview your points. This gives them a clear set of guideposts. The audience also has an attention after-burner adrenaline mode and if you can show them the finish line at the appropriate time, it can reignite their energy.

Some like to make their presentations interactive. Often you can build in a two-way or Q&A element. While it might engage the audience for a moment as a demonstration of your willingness to open the floor, maintaining that connection and your credibility is a tall order. Getting your audience on-board based on an acknowledgement you share their concerns in such a forum is a delicate thing. And if you open your presentation up to questions, you don't know what creatures from Pandora's Box you might unleash. There is also a danger in breaking that speaker's fourth wall, so to speak, as it changes the dynamics of your position in a presentation. It forces you to switch to the role of moderator/arbitrator instead of an authority, which at times can be an awkward pivot and may not play to your strengths. If you think this is absolutely necessary, incorporate it in the design of the presentation. It might be useful to have a designated moderator lead that part of the discussion.

A common form of leadership communication is the presentation/ Town Hall hybrid. These are large gatherings in an auditorium or other big venue. The concept is that the speaker presents some significant news, update or change in business practices and then answers questions from the audience, providing impromptu answers on the spot. Steven had an interesting Town Hall experience. He was hired as the producer for the Town Hall of an executive who had just been promoted to a division president. The newly anointed executive was anxious to show his team that even though he had moved into this very senior role, he was as interested in the concerns of the average employee as he ever had been. Steven strongly warned against such an unregulated forum. While the intention of such an encounter might be to promote greater accessibility, it is still fraught with peril. He knew there was too much uncertainty about his ascension for people to be asking anything more than whether they'd still have jobs. The executive dismissed the notion of pre-written questions for fear it would seem disingenuous and inauthentic.

What he was willing to do was to rehearse with his staff and practise his off-the-cuff remarks to prove he could handle the crowd. The only problem was his staff were afraid of being too harsh in their questions for fear it would upset their new boss so what Steven saw happening was a perfect storm of ego and ego-enablers walking into a buzzsaw of unbridled negativity. Even the staging was wrong: Steven strongly suggested that questions for the Town Hall should be staged with a standing mic in the aisles in a well-lit space so that the questioner would feel some of the pressure of being on-stage. Unfortunately, for time and logistics sake they chose to pass a hand mic around a poorly lit audience that offered visual cover for the questioners.

The presentation itself was slick and well produced – a close visual representation of the sales pitch he had made to his corporate chiefs to get the job in the first place. But when the lights came up on stage and the audience was encouraged to ask questions, it all fell apart. Hidden voices were wondering about consolidation and budget cuts considering the new direction the presentation offered. While some questions were softballs, in maybe a not-so-veiled effort to play up the new boss, two-thirds of the way through the Q&A things turned a bit ugly. Personal stories started to emerge that were around the burning question, 'What does this all mean for me?' Furthermore, people were asking about the rumours that were flying about the campus. The executive was caught off guard, his chance to connect was coopted and his credibility took a big hit.

Now, ideally a Town Hall Q&A should be full of the burning, but hard questions employees have. But, as this exec learned, if you choose to give up the cool safety of the podium, you had better be ready to take the heat from the crowd.

While some members of your audience will take copious notes and hang onto every word as if their jobs depend on it, do not count on it. First of all, you can never predict if the key listeners are paying this kind of close attention and despite feeling that if they are writing they are liking, you really do not know what is in those notes.

A better way to ensure listeners take away what you want them to is to provide your own material. Often called 'leave behinds', these are the notes you wish they would have taken. You won't give these out until after the talk, but it is a good idea to have prepared notes for your audience so they do not have to be concerned about missing your key points. This gives you the strategic advantage of being able to emphasize exactly which points you want remembered. Our advice? Make this your standard practice.

The Eye Candy Store

We purposely leave the discussion of visual element and slides to the end of your planning process. Slides have, unfortunately, become so ubiquitous that a presentation without them feels unfinished so remember this maxim: slides must be visual. Slides must be aids. They should help add clarity to your talk in a way your words cannot.

Before PowerPoint and other slide applications, speakers would write their presentations and then go to the graphic design department to create visual elements. Today, almost everyone does it themselves and few organizations even have graphic departments anymore. This has led to two opposite but equally destructive presentation trends: too many words and too many distracting visuals.

Most slide applications do not limit the number of words that can be put on the slide. Keep adding words and the type just gets smaller and smaller. So, a few rules of thumb. Despite what the program may drive you to do, set your master slide to have content no smaller than 28pt type – better yet, 32. Headers do not need to be larger than 36pt. This will limit the number of words you can put on your slides and that is a good limitation to abide by. Bullets should be just that, succinct, incomplete sentences, and the nugget of your point. No punctuation. Single lines.

Your slides are not your notes. Remember, the audience can read faster than you can speak so when they are reading the slide, they are not listening to you. And, of course, they already know what you are going to say! The bullets should be a kind of high-level summary that will reinforce your points with your listeners. You can, and should, use simple bullets with pictures or graphics – but not at the expense of clarity.

It is far too easy to let pictures, charts and graphs get the better of you. The better you become with developing visuals, the more likely it is you will become enamoured with your efforts and that can lead to overkill. The key is to let the graphics highlight your story, not the other way around. The slides are there to add to the clarity of your points. There is a simple set of rules to follow for your slides:

Fewer words beat lots of words.
Numbers beat words.
Charts and graphs beat numbers
and
Pictures beat charts and graphs.

Following that logic, your slides should provide that which your words cannot do as well. Graphics, imagery and even bullets are powerful tools, but should be used sparingly. Think of them as a powerful spice: the more you use them, the more they will overpower you.

While working for a major entertainment company, Steven coached a newly hired executive with a long and impressive background in live event and theatrical presentation businesses. The entertainment company was looking for new ways to showcase their franchises and live events was a natural extension of these storied productions. The execution had to be handled with extreme care to protect the fan connection with the original properties. This meant the executive had to work closely with, and build the trust of, the top creative studio executives. For the first meeting between this successful executive and the head of the studio, she sought to explain the nuances and opportunities that live events could offer. She also intended to provide history and context for how this had been used effectively by other studios. All very valuable perspective and interesting information.

The executive toiled for weeks working on her slide presentation. She produced a beautiful 37-slide deck that anyone would be proud to deliver. There was only one problem: she had just one hour for the meeting. The underlying mission of the meeting was not to educate the studio chief on live events. Rather, it was to lay the foundation for building trust with the studio chief. Demonstrating an understanding of the studio chief's concerns was necessary, demonstrating proficiency with graphics was not. Steven took one look at the 37 slides and got out his red pen. Within minutes, he had reduced their number to 15 and pared down her talk to a story that could be told in 20 minutes. The remaining 40 minutes would be a conversation. That reassessed strategy paid dividends to that executive for years and Steven came to be known as 'The PowerPoint Slasher', a nickname he wears proudly to this day.

Practice Doesn't Make Perfect – It Makes You

A speaker provides the nuance and relevance of their talk through their authenticity and personality. The way to master this is practice. Practice does not mean trying to mimic a presenter you admire. That is fruitless. The key to achieving credible presentation communication is practising so your natural personality shows through. This results in you looking and feeling more confident as you build your credibility delivering a convincing message. The more your listeners believe you and trust the authenticity of your message, the less likely they will be judgemental of you and your talk. That is not to say people will necessarily just accept what you have to say, but they will find their judgements tempered based on their respect for your arguments and the credibility capital you bring. It's an interesting circle of strengths and emotions: the lower your confidence, the more scrutiny you are likely to feel. The greater your confidence, the more command you have of a situation. That command and presence can be achieved only with practice.

For most, practice may simply come in the form of repetition. The number of times you may tell a story has a lot to do with the ease and comfort you have in telling that story to make a point. Once you have told a story 30 or 40 times, you have a pretty clear idea of what parts of the story resonate and what parts should be jettisoned because they get in the way of making your point. Your credibility is at your highest when you demonstrate your command of the language and the narrative. Unfortunately, most communication we are assigned to deliver doesn't afford us the luxury of time and repetition so we must find our own unique ways to be as efficient with our practice as possible. There is no one-size-fits-all approach and different communication situations require different methods of practice, but finding your personal formula is truly the key.

Tooling Your Practice

Don't skimp on your commitment – sacrifice any of these phases at your own risk. Universally, those who put the time into something will be more successful at it. Malcom Gladwell's *Outliers* book is popular in part because it called out 10,000 hours of practice necessary to achieve mastery.[1] And while no one expects you to chalk up that number of hours practising for a presentation, think of it as a cumulative effect of practising for many presentations. You might be surprised how close you get to both the number and mastery.

When training to deliver convincing messaging, executives and actors often want to know what the 'tricks' are. Everyone always asks, 'Should I memorize what I have to say?' 'Should I use 3x5 index cards?' 'Should I ask for a teleprompter?' 'Should I just read over my notes a few times and just wing it?' There is of course no single answer for every encounter. Like so many things, there are topics each of us have a proclivity to retain which require little prompting. That said, here is a process that works for most people when giving a presentation: start with paragraphs and end with triggers. The best trigger notes will be those that stimulate a chain of thoughts with the material you need to cover.

So, with the goal of delivering what appears to be an extemporaneous, passionate and confident message, what are the tools at your disposal? First, let's take the most arduous and difficult method off the table – memorization. Leave memorizing to the actors who are working with carefully crafted scripts. Even if you are a great writer, the odds that you can deliver your prose with the same thoughtfulness as a professional are slim. Don't let yourself be frustrated by trying to accomplish the impossible. The best way for most people to deliver a convincing message is to work with trigger notes.

Trigger notes give you the key elements of the talk in the order you determined to be most effective: they literally trigger the thoughts in your head and then out come the words. This is effective because it is the way human beings speak naturally. We don't communicate words in conversations, we communicate thoughts. Finding just the right words is much less important than finding the right thoughts. This gives your talk a conversational quality that lets your personality, authenticity and authority shine through.

The amount of detail in your trigger notes depends on how much specific information you need to present. Statistics, technicalities, dates should be included. You don't want to risk getting them wrong. Concepts, advocacy and reasoning just need a trigger word to remind

---

[1]Gladwell, Malcolm (2011), *Outliers: The Story of Success*, New York: Back Bay Books.

you of the points you want to make. As you practise, you will become more comfortable with both the facts and figures and the use of trigger words.

The more important the talk, the more important it is to rehearse in front of people, so don't let the first time you go start-to-finish with a critical presentation be in the real thing. Find an impartial but supportive audience for your dress rehearsal. Finding the right blend of support and criticism can be a challenge, but if you really want to advance your competence, it is essential. You want supportive people who will give you constructive feedback. Co-workers, family, friends may all be appropriate in different circumstances with different topics.

Try to practise in an environment that best simulates the situation in which you will be speaking. Don't do it sitting down. Use a high table or a music stand as a substitute for a lectern. Standing up changes both physical energy and mental focus. The more real you make the experience of delivering your talk, the better sense you will have of how successfully you are delivering it. After each practice, take questions from your faux audience. Practising impromptu Q&A is just as important as rehearsing the talk itself. While they may be unfamiliar with your topic and its specifics, you want any and all questions on substance. It will make the real thing a whole lot more comfortable.

When it is time for feedback, listen carefully. You want to know how the introduction came across, whether or not your jokes were funny. How did you use your body? Did you gesture? Did you stand straight? Did you demonstrate command of the space? Did you just seem generally comfortable? You want them to point out areas where the flow of the talk might have been a touch awkward or confusing. Basically, you want to assess how well you held their attention, and why.

Working with a Teleprompter
Sometimes, when presenting a formal, written-out speech to a large group, the only way to do it is with a teleprompter (autocue). This is a device that projects your text onto a clear screen that looks like clear glass to the audience. It scrolls through your talk as you speak. These are excellent tools in the right situation, but they require practice. You cannot improvise. You have to deliver the words as written, or the operator may well lose your place. You have to practise with the

operator so they learn your pacing. This is the person who will be responsible for this complex technology and you do not want to begin building the relationship at the last minute.

A few suggestions if you find yourself working with a teleprompter. First, if you have only one screen, it will be in front of you. Don't stare at it. Catch a few words ahead and deliver them to the audience at your left or right. Practising will make this easier. Ideally, you have the more desirable configuration of three screens, one each on the left, right and centre. When you move from one to another, do not do it just by moving your eyes. That looks a bit creepy and evokes the phrase 'shifty-eyed'. Instead, move your whole head and your body slightly. It makes you look far more natural and simulates looking at the audience. One of the other challenges with prompters is remembering to take pauses or emphasis. Use symbols to remind you. A backward slash/ can mean pause. Underline can mean emphasize. A double slash// can indicate a longer pause.

Rebecca once worked with the CEO of a Fortune 500 company who was delivering a major address to the leaders of the company. It was a large and geographically diverse organization and he had to give it four times. He used a teleprompter pretty well when Rebecca began to work with him. After the first presentation, she sensed that he was stepping on a lot of applause lines – it was a good time for the company and it was an upbeat and powerful talk. Additionally, a few laugh lines surprised him and he did not wait long enough for the laughter to die down. When she met with him in preparation for the next and largest audience, she told him this. He did not have a feeling for reading the audience to anticipate the reaction. She worked on the speech and put in symbols for pauses where she expected the applause lines. There were six.

When he gave the next speech, he received all six applause lines plus a couple of others because he was learning to sense the audience's reactions.

Rebecca met with him a few days later. Leaning back in his chair, with his hands behind his head, he said, 'So, does this feel like *Pygmalion?*' She smiled and said that yes, it did. He never stepped on an applause line or a laugh line again.

There are a lot of stories of teleprompter disasters. One of the most notable came in September 1993 when President Bill Clinton was delivering an address on healthcare, or at least he thought that was what he was giving. Somehow, an eight-month-old economic policy address was loaded into the teleprompter computer instead. Clinton, master communicator that he was, pressed ahead on the correct topic without a detectable hiccup. As you can imagine, his staff was in full-on panic mode. The President finally got the correct text of the speech a full seven minutes into his talk.

We reiterate this story for two reasons. First, to point out a reliance on technology is fraught with peril. Second, practising and knowing your talk inside and out will help if glitches occur. So, unless you want to make the commitment to learning and practising with this specific tool, pass on this not-so-easy fix.

The Aftermath

People rarely talk about the post-presentation period, so focused are they on surviving the talk itself. It is, however, something to think about. There are two factors at play that influence it. One is the emotional high of a well-received talk that accomplished its goal. And two, once the horse has left the barn, it's harder to corral its attention again. So how will you keep your key points in your audience's mind going forward?

The letdown effect from a particularly stressful run up to a presentation is real. The release of stress hormones after a consequential talk is real and sometimes results in emotional and physical symptoms. For most people, however, the transition back to normal is a bit less intense, but no less real. Generally, it is a combination of mental and physical exhaustion followed by performance self-analysis.[2] So, the question is, how do you come down from the mountain you have worked so hard to climb? The key is to manage the stress during the process, not wait until the event has concluded. Maintaining your exercise regimen, eating properly and even doing brief, off-topic mental activities like a crossword puzzle will give your mind and body

[2]Grayson Mathis, Charlotte E. (2002), 'Suffering From "Let-Down Effect?"', WebMD, https://www.webmd.com/men/features/suffering-from-let-down-effect

a pause from the stress of an upcoming presentation. And, when self-analysing, be kind to yourself.[3][4][5] After all, we are all our own worst and unfriendly critics!

CONCLUSION

Every time you prepare and give a talk, remember that you are unlikely to be judged on the exact words used. People don't remember the words, they remember the concepts and how you made them feel. They judge your credibility and other factors such as tone, visual cues, enthusiasm, authenticity and demeanour. Above all, what speaks to your credibility is the style and ease with which you present the material. They look to see you demonstrate confidence and resilience. It is not about having all the answers. Rather, it is about demonstrating your understanding of the expanse of the issue, the problems associated with it and how you address challenges. A bit of humility lives hand-in-hand with your confidence and the two together will greatly increase your ability to connect with an audience.

Finally, it may sound funny to say, but you should also make the effort not to miss your own talk. It is a privilege and an honour to be asked to speak, no matter what the occasion – people do want to hear what you have to say and you should enjoy that privilege. Don't make your speech an out-of-body experience. Come from a place of connecting with your audience. That is real mastery. Then, and only then, will you have succeeded in taking the focus off yourself and shifted it to your listeners and the impact your words can have upon them. This is the place from which memorable change is made and you will make the greatest lasting impression. And that is what builds long-lasting credibility capital.

[3]Mayo Clinic (accessed 28 April 2021), 'Exercise and Stress: Get Moving to Manage Stress', https://www.mayoclinic.org/healthy-lifestyle/stress-management/in-depth/exercise-and-stress/art-20044469

[4]Rizzolo, Denise et al. (10 January 2011), 'Stress Management Strategies For Students: The Immediate Effects Of Yoga, Humour, And Reading On Stress', *Journal of College Teaching & Learning (TLC)* 6, No. 8, https://doi.org/10.19030/tlc.v6i8.1117

[5]Parker-Pope, Tara 'How to Be Better at Stress', https://www.nytimes.com/guides/well/how-to-deal-with-stress

Index

Note: page numbers in **bold** refer to diagrams, page numbers in *italics* refer to information contained in tables and questionnaires.